THE POACHER'S LAWYER

Written & illustrated by Hunter Adair

Chancery House Press
15 Wickham Road, Beckenham
Kent, BR3 5JS, England

Copyright © 2005   Hunter Adair

All rights reserved   No part of this book may be reproduced, stored in a retrieval system, or transmitted in any form or by any means, electronic, mechanical, photocopying, recording or otherwise, without the express written permission of the publishers.

ISBN   0 900246 90 1

Published by   Chancery House Press
15 Wickham Road
Beckenham
Kent
BR3 5JS
England

Price   £10.99

By the same author

Muck Spreadin'
Shooting and the Countryside
Mucky Boots
The Mucky Road to Tongue Farm
The Four Seasons in the North
Thompsons of Prudhoe the First 50 Years
A Guide to the Countryside

Books for Children

Stone Walls
Clydesdale Horses
Fruits, Flowers & Shrubs
Farm Animals & Farming
Wild Birds & Animals
Hay & Harvest Time
Farm Buildings & Milking Parlours
People Who Live & Work in the Countryside
Farming in the North
Some Wildlife Secrets - in preparation

Also published by Chancery House Press

The Hangman's Record. Vol I .1868-1899
The Hangman's Record. Vol II 1900-1929
The Hangman's Record. Vol III 1930-1964
Adhesive Wafer Seals – a Transient Victorian Phenomenon

CONTENTS

	INTRODUCTION	iv
Chapter 1	THE SPORTING RIGHTS	1
Chapter 2	BOUNDARY FENCES	13
Chapter 3	DUCKS & THE FORESHORE	26
Chapter 4	THE SPORTSMAN & HIS DOG	41
Chapter 5	CAN ANYONE SHOOT GROUND GAME WITHOUT A LICENCE?	56
Chapter 6	POACHING	72
Chapter 7	DEER	87
Chapter 8	ROOKS	105
Chapter 9	TRESPASSING	118
Chapter 10	CLOSE TIMES, MANORS & WARRENS	134

INTRODUCTION

The countryside is a marvellous place to be involved with; it provides work, sporting activities, education, beauty and a livelihood for many people who live and work there.

More and more people from the towns and cities are now wanting to spend part of their leisure time in the countryside and those with the money also want a share in the sporting facilities.

Many people from all walks of life now take part in the country sports every year. At one time it was only the landowners and the aristocrats that enjoyed the hunting, shooting and fishing in the countryside.

Things are changing in the countryside, although the old feudal system is still in place. The people from the towns and cities bring new money into the countryside which is badly needed and many landowners need this new money to keep their estates and lands together.

Nothing is really certain about the law except for the costs. This book is full of tales from an old sporting solicitor's book from the beginning of the last century. I have put some of the tales into layman's terms so that they will be easy to understand and follow. There are some very humorous tales and many of the old laws made in the 1800's are still the law today.

I have also included throughout the book stories about how my father taught me all about the laws and animals of the countryside and how he dealt with poachers.

As the law is changing all the time this cannot be considered a legally binding publication and the author and publishers take no responsibility for the information contained herein.

Chapter 1   THE SPORTING RIGHTS

The countryside is a lovely place to live and be brought up in, as there are many natural, simple things that go on in the countryside every day which you would never see in the city.

For instance the other evening a friend and I were standing out in the farm garden looking over the fence at about twenty young lambs playing in the field.

It was a nice evening although there was a bit of a chill in the air. The young lambs were running along the side of the boundary fence for about thirty yards as fast as they could run. Then suddenly they would all stop and turn round and then come galloping back along the side of the fence at full speed.

The young lambs kept running backwards and forwards for about twenty minutes before splitting up and dashing back to their mothers for a deserved drink of milk. It was a delightful sight watching these young lambs playing, although I see some wonderful things in the countryside nearly every day. However, simple things, like watching young lambs playing, are very enjoyable.

My father used to tell us boys, when we were young, that it wasn't a bad thing to own a part of the old countryside. He always said buying a bit of the countryside was like having an insurance policy for old age.

Being the owner of a bit of land can have its problems. The more land that some families own, the more they are inclined to let some of their land out to other people at a cost. The land may be let out to tenant farmers, or for shooting over, or for caravans.

There are many different types of functions and sports for which land is leased or rented out in this country. Landowners make all sorts of rent agreements with people for a small or large bit of land.

This book is full of tales from the countryside and from the foreshore, about the laws of the land. There have been many court battles in the past to sort out who has the right to what from the soil and the rights to the land and the shore.

When you walk into the countryside or you rent some land from a farmer to shoot over it, then what rights do you really have? Many laws made at the beginning of the century still stand today. Some of the cases and stories which I will try and explain simply to you how they came about and the outcome, will certainly amuse and surprise you.

So let me first kick off by talking about the sporting rights on land. The rights over land of any description is what the law calls *incorporeal hereditaments* and as a result they can only be granted or assigned by deed. That is, by a document which contains proper words of grant and which is sealed, as well as being signed.

The sporting rights can be granted separately, you do not need to own the land; but they can only be granted officially by deed. The landowner can reserve the sporting rights for himself if he lets the land out whether the letting is effected by agreement in writing or verbally.

Let me give you a simple example as to what can

happen. A landowner has the sporting rights assigned to him by deed on the land which he owns. He then lets the sporting rights over the land to a small syndicate called group B; but not under seal.

Later the landowner also decides to let the sporting rights over the same land to another small syndicate called group C in the same year. Group C can shoot game over the land in the face of the B group and the B group can't do a thing about it.

The reason why the B group cannot do a thing about the C group shooting game over the land, which they have also paid for the sporting rights, is simply because group B hadn't the sporting rights granted to them over the land by deed. It was only a verbal agreement, or an agreement by letter, which wouldn't have made the slightest difference.

The landowner with the sporting rights can let his land out to a farmer, or to anyone for grazing or for keeping ponies. The landowner can reserve the sporting rights over the land for his family and friends. If, say, the farmer, or his son, is then caught shooting game on the land he has rented, he can be prosecuted for trespass and he can also be tossed off his farm.

It is very rare indeed that a landowner will let the sporting rights over his land to two groups of people in the same year, but this has happened in the past and could happen again.

Now let me turn to fox hunting. I am a game shooting man myself and whilst I am still interested in foxes and fox hunting I didn't follow any particular fox hunt on a regular basis.

Hunting foxes with dogs was banned in England and Wales in February 2005.

Some of my country friends followed their local fox hounds and they got a great deal of pleasure from following the hounds and seeing them running well. They also get a great deal of pleasure from just seeing a fox.

The fox more often escaped because it knew the terrain and would very often lose the hounds. Man is a born hunter, whether some people like it or not, and fox hunting has a long history where farmers and landowners have chased and hunted foxes to try and stop them from killing their poultry and lambs.

Many people are against fox hunting, they think it is a cruel, barbaric sport. I fully understand their point of view and concern about fox hunting, but I don't entirely agree with them.

Foxes are vermin and need to be controlled and I am not sure how people intend to control foxes. Shooting foxes is not an easy job as the fox is not silly enough to let somebody get close enough to have a pot shot at it.

If shooting was the only method of controlling foxes there would be more wounded foxes running about the countryside suffering a lot of pain because of man's stupidity. Trapping foxes would cause the same thing to happen, as most of the foxes that were trapped would have to suffer a lot more pain than any foxes that were caught and killed instantly by fox hounds.

Gassing foxes is probably the safest way of killing them. It is silent and it is clean. The problem here is that many foxes and badgers use the same entrance to their lying-up quarters. I could see the badger population being greatly reduced with the foxes if gassing replaces fox hunting. That maybe wouldn't be a bad thing as there are far too many badgers anyway.

I sometimes wonder if some of the general public were simply against the people that hunted on horse back and a bit of sour grapes was attached to their thinking. Wanting to ban fox hunting was just a way of getting at these so called "snobs" who follow the hounds on horse back and on foot. This is nonsense as people from all walks of life hunted.

Maybe these people did not think that some of the alternative methods for controlling foxes could cause more pain to the foxes than hunting them with fox hounds.

What right has anyone got to go galloping over another man's land with horses chasing after a fox anyway? Are they not trespassing?

When fox hunting was perfectly lawful it was thought for many years, and still is by some people, that anyone had the right to follow a pack of hounds over another man's land without his permission. This was not the case.

As far back as 1786 an interesting case was tried in the Court of King's Bench where a group were sued for trespass for hunting a fox over another man's land.

The group pleaded that they were hunting the fox to stop it from doing mischief in the neighbourhood and that was the only method of killing it. This was held to be a good plea and the person failed in his action for trespass.

It has subsequently often been held, that although one may perhaps justify following a fox over another man's land, there is absolutely no excuse for a bunch of horses and a group of foot men to follow fox hounds over anyone's land without permission, at any time of the year.

Wild birds and animals such as foxes and pheasants are annexed to the soil and belong to no one while they are alive and free.

Annexed to the soil means they are on top of the soil and can move about freely from one man's land to another man's land. They are different from domesticated birds and animals which cannot escape freely.

The milk quota for instance was introduced into the U.K. in 1984. The quota that each dairy farmer was allocated was the amount of milk that they had produced the previous year in 1983.

But the milk quota is annexed to the land and doesn't belong to the dairy farmer or landowner, they only have the use of the quota. This caused lots of problems at first and it still does on some farms, as the dairy farmers that produce the milk think the milk quota belongs to them. But it belongs to nobody.

The milk quota is annexed to the land, as are wild birds and animals. There are many differences between the milk quota and the wild birds and animals in the countryside, but I won't go into any further details about the milk quota. I just wanted to explain to you how the milk quota and the wild birds and animals don't belong to anyone as they just lie on top of the soil. (See also milk quota in chapter 9).

THE WOODCOCK

As I have said, wild birds and animals don't belong to anybody when they are alive and free. It is only at the point where they are captured or killed that the ownership of the wild bird or animal can be established.

Generally speaking, however, an estate that rears young pheasants for the sport of shooting on the estate and who have the sporting rights on the estate, will own the pheasants that they are rearing.

Let me now give you another simple example of who the pheasants really belong to by law and why. Even if you rear pheasants on your estate, or you buy in young pheasants as poults and rear them on for the sport of shooting, you own them.

I walked onto Farmer A's land with my gun and dog, the dog flushed a pheasant which I had two shots at and only clipped its wing, the pheasant flew on.

I followed the pheasant onto Farmer B's land where the dog flushed the bird again. This time I shot the bird stone dead with one shot (just luck).

Who do you think the pheasant belongs to? The pheasant doesn't belong to Farmer A because he didn't follow the pheasant from his land and it doesn't belong to Farmer B because it wasn't started on his land.

Funnily enough the pheasant belongs to me because I shot it. But hold on a bit my dear friend, both Farmer A. and Farmer B. can have me for trespass in pursuit of game.

If a poacher, for instance, kills and takes game on Farmer A's land which he found there and had not flushed it from Farmer B's land then the game belongs to Farmer A and the poacher is in serious trouble.

There is, however, a so-called special right of property. If Farmer A starts game on his own land, follows it and kills it on Farmer B's land, the game will belong to Farmer A. At the same time Farmer A has no right to follow game onto Farmer B's land and kill it. He is committing an offence and can be prosecuted for it.

Hare coursing or hunting with beagles is another country sport which was very unpopular with some people. As long as the hare had a chance to escape, and they all did, then more often than not they did escape.

It is the thought of the hare being caught by the beagles and being torn to pieces by the hounds that put some people against the sport. The hare was not normally torn to pieces, they were usually killed instantly when, and if, they were caught and they didn't suffer any pain what so ever.

It was very often customary to give, or offer, any killed hares to the occupier of the land on which they were killed; but this was just a matter of courtesy only and not a right, unless the hare was started and killed on the same man's land.

The hare that had been started on one man's land and killed, or taken alive on another man's land, belonged to the person in charge of the hunt at the time.

Occasionally a spectator at the hunt was able to take and catch a spent, or tired hare, in front of the hounds. Assuming the hare was started on a farm, other than on the one on which it was caught, then the question of who the hare belonged to would depend a great deal on what the spectator's intentions were.

If the spectator took the hare for the benefit of the huntsman and handed the hare over to him to be killed, it belonged to the huntsman, but if the spectator caught the hare in order to spite the hunters, the hare belonged to the spectator.

If on the other hand the hare was killed on the same farm as that on which it was started, then the hare did not belong to the huntsman, nor did it belong to the spectator. It belonged to the farmer, or to the person having the sporting rights over the farm. Hunting hares with dogs was also banned in England and Wales in February 2005.

I don't know if you have ever had hare soup, marvellous stuff on a cold day and it doesn't half stick to your ribs. My mother was a great soup maker. When my father shot a hare and brought it home from the fields, he would hang it up for a couple of days then my mother would skin it and chop the meat into pieces.

My mother put lumps of potato in hare soup along with lumps of the meat, she also added peas, lentils and barley; she partly cooked the hare first then the rest of the ingredients were added and the soup was simmered until the meat was tender.

If you had two plates of my mother's home made hare soup at lunch time you didn't need much more to eat for the rest of that day. Come to think about it, all her soups were a meal on their own and her soups had a delicious flavour.

Now, some nice little questions as to who the game belongs to when you are shooting along the borders on your estate, or your farm and the question of any trespass. There has been many a heated debate, over lunch on a shooting day, as to whether such a dead bird on the game cart belongs to the host, or, to the neighbour over the border.

The border could just be an open ditch with no fence. To give you a practical example. One of Mr A's guests said he shot a pheasant and it fell on Mr B's land. Watching the shooting was B's gamekeeper to see that none of his pheasants were shot. He calmly picked up the pheasant and walked off with it.

Could the guest who shot the pheasant go round to B's gamekeeper and claim the pheasant as belonging to Mr A? Guest number two said that it would depend on whether it was dead when the gamekeeper picked it up.

Guest number three said that it doesn't, it all depends on whether it was dead when it struck the ground. Whilst Guest number four doesn't pretend to know much about it, but he thinks that if the question depends on when the bird died, the time to consider would be when the pheasant crossed over the boundary, was it flying then, or was it dead and simply falling?

Mr A had been listening in silence to some of his guests having the heated debate on to whom the pheasant belonged. He then turned to another of his guests that day, who was his learned friend *The Poacher's Lawyer* and asked him for his opinion on the pheasant.

The Poacher's Lawyer, with the caution instilled into him by his legal training, said, 'The point is by no means an easy one to decide on.' As far as he can remember it has never been before a High Court, at least he thinks there is no reported case.

The lawyer went on to say, 'If the bird was dead when the gamekeeper picked it up, there is no doubt that the pheasant belongs to Mr A. If it was only tipped in the wing and it would have got away, if the gamekeeper had not been on the spot and had been too quick for the pheasant, or if it required the keeper's dog to catch it, the pheasant would belong to Mr B. If the pheasant was not quite dead when the gamekeeper picked it up, but was mortally wounded, then it is rather doubtful to whom it belongs. I think it is legally A's bird.'

Whilst tucking into beef pie and bottled beer, Mr A said, 'That's all very well old chap, but what are your reasons for your verdict?'

The Poacher's Lawyer said with a smile, after consuming a few bottles of beer, 'My reason is that in order to acquire a property in such things as game you must, as we lawyers say, reduce them into possession. It is a popular fallacy to suppose you must absolutely kill them if you catch a bird alive, but if you so wound it, that it can't get away and you can go at any moment and pick it up, then you have reduced it into possession. Therefore, if the bird was so wounded that it couldn't run away, when Mr B's gamekeeper picked it up, then the bird belonged to

Mr A. However, if the bird was a runner and would have required the gamekeeper's dog to go after it and pick it up, then the bird will belong to Mr B.'

The guest of Mr A who shot the bird, said he thought it was stone dead after he shot it. The lying sod. I hear that story often enough from game shooters.

While I am sitting at my desk writing up these notes, at 10.00 o'clock at night, I am sipping a glass of sloe-gin which I made. It is a lovely smooth drink. This is about the best gin I have made, it is five years old and has nice rich red colour.

I make two or three bottles of sloe-gin every year. It is a lovely drink just to have a sip of on a cold day, when you are out shooting. It is also a nice after-dinner drink when you have friends around.

It is very easy to make. Take one cup of sloes and one cup of sugar. Prick the sloes with a fork and put them into a large bottle - any sort of bottle - and add the sugar. Then pour in a bottle of White Satin gin and keep mixing for a few days until the sugar is dissolved. Then store in a cupboard for a few months when it will be ready for drinking. (Sweet Dreams).

"Runners", which are wounded birds and animals, are another subject that cause many a debate on the shooting field and they can make enemies between gamekeepers and the owners of game shoots. A bit of give and take is normally the best practice, when you have two shoots joining one another.

There is no problem sending a dog after a runner on your own shoot, you don't break any laws by doing this but, is it justifiable to send your dog after a runner onto another man's land?

No it is not, you are committing a trespass if you wilfully send your dog after a runner, or a wounded bird, onto another man's land. Apart from the trespass, the game when retrieved will belong to the shooter, at least, it will if it was followed by the dog at once on the day of the shoot.

The next day after a game shoot Mr A's gamekeeper goes round his shoot to pick up any lost, or wounded, birds. His dog follows a runner from his master's wood over the boundary into Mr B's wood and retrieves the runner. The bird will belong to Mr A.

There could be an action of trespass here if the gamekeeper actually sent the dog across the boundary after the runner. On the other hand what if Mr A's gamekeeper saw a wounded bird on the neighbour's land and sent his dog over the boundary to pick it up?

Mr A would have no right to this bird if his gamekeeper's dog retrieved it. No matter how certain he might be that it was one of the birds shot, on his own shoot, the previous day. He is committing a trespass in pursuit of game.

Remember where two shoots join each other it is always best to avoid any unpleasantness with your neighbours. It is better all round to have an understanding with each other on the boundaries of your shoot and to have a bit of give and take.

There is an old saying that Hunting makes friends and shooting makes enemies. There is no truer saying which I am, reluctantly, compelled to admit.

Chapter 2   BOUNDARY FENCES

Nothing perhaps creates more discussion and disputes between sportsmen than the questions arising from the rights of shooting boundary fences or hedges.

There are a lot of game shooters who are used to doubling their boundary fences when they are out shooting. In plain English this means walking on the far side (the neighbour's side of the fence).

The various pheasant shoots I go to every year have a great variety of boundary fences, hedges, walls, ditches, rivers and woods. Sometimes at a shoot someone will walk over the boundary fence either hunting for game or they will stand on another man's land when one of their own woods is being driven to them.

They may find that by standing on another man's land they have a better chance of getting a shot on a certain pheasant drive. The shooter may think that nobody will mind as they are not doing any harm, but they will mind, as the shooter is trespassing.

It is also quite a common thing for some shooters to walk onto another man's land when they are walking along boundary fences. Sending dogs onto another man's land is more common because the dog owner thinks that nobody will see him, or they won't be caught and some of them think they are not doing any harm. They are, they are trespassing.

Most shooters know that they shouldn't be walking on another man's land, but they are not sure as to what extent they are breaking the law and some shooters are quite willing to walk onto another man's land and say nothing to anybody.

I have been caught on another man's land with my gun and dog with other people when I was a guest at a pheasant shoot in the Scottish Borders. I was asked what the hell I was doing on their land by a very angry lady. So I explained to this angry lady that I was just a guest at the shoot and I was sorry, but I didn't know I was trespassing on her land

The lady quickly calmed down with me and she turned quite pleasant, I was just standing over the boundary, but she was still very aggressive with the other shooters who were walking further through her wood hunting for game and she kept shouting at them to get to hell off her land.

I felt quite embarrassed at the time as I was only invited to the pheasant shoot as a guest that day and to be approached by a lady and asked what the hell I was doing on her land was a bit off-putting to say the least.

When we all got off her land none of the other shooters seemed to be all that bothered about the lady. I over-heard one of the regular shooters saying she is always complaining about something or another.

What does the law have to say about boundary fences, ditches and game birds? Let me give you a simple example of what the position is regarding boundary hedges, game birds and ditches.

Has Farmer A a right to walk on his neighbour's side of the fence when he is shooting the boundary hedge? No such right exists.

Farmer A shoots a pheasant which falls onto Farmer B's land. Who do you think the pheasant belongs to? Depending where the bird was killed will decide who it belongs to.

If for instance the pheasant was killed on Farmer A's land, but fell on Farmer B's land the pheasant will belong to Farmer A. On the other hand if Farmer A kills the bird when it is over the boundary hedge, then the bird belongs to Farmer B.

Remember wild birds and animals are not the property of anyone while they are alive and free. It is only at the point where the bird or animal is caught or killed can they be claimed.

A number of sportsmen think that if the ditch is on the opposite side of the hedge to the land over which he has the shooting he has the right to the game and also the right to walk the brow of the ditch.

It is also frequently thought that the owner of the hedge or ditch is entitled to four or six feet of land from the stub of the hedge. This four or six feet is just country folklore in some areas.

The rule about ditching is this. No man making a ditch can cut into his neighbour's soil, but usually cuts to the very extremity of his own land.

He is of course bound to throw the soil which he digs out upon his own land and if he likes he can plant a hedge on the top of the soil. No rule about four or six feet has anything to with it, a point of law decided upon in 1810, and still stands today.

If Farmer A shoots a pheasant which falls into the middle of a boundary hedge the bird can belong to either Farmer A or B.

Boundary hedges are very complicated. If Farmer B allows Farmer A to walk on his land while shooting the boundary hedge and vice-versa it's probably because they think they have this right.

I hope it is now becoming a bit clearer to you what rights you have when you are out shooting game on your own land or on a friend's land. I am trying to make the law as simple and easy to understand and follow as I can.

Now let me tell you a true story about a landowner and a boundary hedge. This story which I think is very funny and amusing, just highlights the problems that can arise from boundary hedges.

One Monday morning, many years ago, this well known landowner walked into the office of *The Poacher's Lawyer*, where he was greeted by the lawyer. The landowner burst out with, 'I have been insulted by a man who used to polish my father's boots. Such insolence I have received from this man and I have come to you to put a stop to it.' The lawyer said, 'Who is this man that insulted you and what has he done?'

The landowner said, 'I beg your pardon, I forgot myself for a moment; a month ago I was shooting the boundary hedge with some friends and I sent my gamekeeper over to double a fence and walk on the other side of the hedge. The ditch was on the other side of the hedge and I sent my gamekeeper over to walk along the brow of the ditch. The neighbour's stockman saw my gamekeeper walking the brow of the ditch and he told him to get to hell off his land. The gamekeeper jumped back over to my side of the hedge.'

The landowner went on, 'Then this past Saturday I was shooting the boundary fence again with some friends and this time I said I would walk along the brow of the ditch on the other side of the hedge. When the neighbour's stockman appeared again. The stockman told me to get bloody well off their land. I took no notice of the stockman and carried on walking along the brow of the ditch. Then suddenly the stockman walked forward and pushed me into the ditch. He also took my gun off me and flung it over the hedge onto my own land.'

The landowner continued his tale and said, 'The stockman went on, "Now bloody well get back over the hedge or I will put you over." The stockman was a big fellow and I just did what he told me. I now want to claim damages from him.'

'Hold on.' said the lawyer, 'in the first place you were trespassing, when you were walking along the brow of the ditch on the other side of your boundary hedge and you had no right to be there.'

The landowner then said, 'My dear sir, are you saying what I have cherished from my boyhood, and what I got from my father and he from his father before him, that the owner of a boundary hedge is entitled to four feet in width from the stub of the hedge is a fallacy?'

The landowner continued, 'The ditch, remember, is only a bare three feet wide. I had it measured carefully. My father before me has always had the hedge cut and the ditch cleaned out and my men have always gone onto the neighbour's land to do this work nearly every year.'

The lawyer said, 'That may be very well, but I am sorry to have to tell you that you have been trespassing on your neighbour's land when you are walking along the brow of the ditch on his side of the hedge.'

'Very well,' said the landowner, 'but I must obtain satisfaction for the brutal outrage committed on me by the neighbour's stockman. Do you recommend a summons for assault or an action to claim damages against the stockman?'

The lawyer said to the landowner, 'My dear sir, I would advise that you take no action against the neighbour's stockman as you were clearly in the wrong.'

The landowner said, 'But I shall be the laughing stock of the whole district, if not the whole county, when they hear what has happened to me.' As the landowner rose from his chair he politely said to the lawyer, 'Good morning, sir,' as he made for the office door.

'Hold on a minute, my dear sir,' said the lawyer to the landowner. 'I shall give you some further information on the matter which may help you to understand the facts better.'

If, for instance, there is no ditch at all, or where there is a ditch on each side of the hedge and it cannot be shown by law to whom the hedges or ditches originally belong to, then the ownership of the hedge or ditch is proved by the exercise of the acts of ownership, such as a person cutting and clipping the hedge, repairing the gaps and cleaning out the ditches.

Whoever has exercised these acts of ownership for an unknown length of time can claim the ownership of the hedge or ditch. It often happens that half the length of a hedge bounding a field belongs to land on one side and the other half of the land to the other.'

The landowner was silently listening to the lawyer as he went on to say, 'And finally, where a fence or a hedge is common property between two lands just as a wall or a hedge is between two houses and is a party wall or hedge.

In such a case the game in the hedge belongs to one equally as much as the other and whoever kills it or secures it first is entitled to it. Either party for instance may catch a runner or a wounded rabbit in such a hedge whichever side it was shot on.'

The landowner said to the lawyer, as he left the office, 'Thank you very much for your advice, but I am very annoyed that I can't take revenge against the neighbour's stockman for the abuse and impudence he gave me.'

When the landowner left the lawyer's office. *The Poacher's Lawyer* turned to a junior in his office and said, 'How the mighty have fallen. He will certainly be the laughing stock among the farm workers and the gamekeepers in the area,' and so he was.

Now let me turn to something a little lighter for a moment and tell you about a gundog which I have at the present time. When this gundog is working in top gear in the field he just goes on and on then suddenly he just keels over and has a fit.

No, it was not an epileptic fit that the dog was having, as was first thought by me and some of my shooting friends. It is a very distressing thing to see when a dog is having a fit and you feel so helpless as you really can't do much to help, but to make the dog as comfortable as possible.

This is a pedigree English springer spaniel puppy which I bought from a breeder who takes his dogs and works them at gundog trials, as well as working them in the shooting field among game birds. The ten-week old puppy was well bred and should have had the makings of a top quality gundog. I paid £80 for the puppy in the summer of 1989.

I started training the young puppy straight away. It was a dog, and when it was a year old I took him out to work on a pheasant shoot, near the end of the season, when there were few pheasants about.

The young dog worked his heart out in top gear all morning. Later on in the afternoon at the end of a pheasant drive, I noticed he was staggering a bit and when I called him to me with the whistle he never seemed to hear the whistle, he just stood and looked at me.

As the dog and I were walking to the next pheasant drive, which was only a short distance away, I just happened to turn round and there he was lying on his side having a fit.

I gave the dog a gentle massage as he was having the fit, which lasted for about two minutes. The dog was very distressed and I got him to the Vets that afternoon, but nothing seemed to be amiss. The dog's heart was alright and the Vet thought the dog was just exhausted and this was his method of telling me he had had enough.

When the dog had another fit several months later when I was working him in some rough ground one fairly hot evening, I thought it was time I had him properly looked at by the Vet.

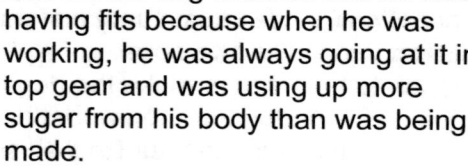

The result of the checks on the dog showed that he was having fits because when he was working, he was always going at it in top gear and was using up more sugar from his body than was being made.

The dog was just exhausted from the lack of sugar and so collapsed and went into a fit. I then had to start and try and manage the dog's rate of work when we were out shooting.

This is not as easy as it seems as the dog is always raring to go in top gear. I also decided to give the dog some extra sugar, when he was out working in the field, to try and stop him having a fit. This was much easier to do than trying to steady the dog down.

Mars bars are what I gave the dog when he was out working in the field, it's a quick supply of sugar. I gave the dog one Mars bar in the morning before we set off shooting. Then during the mid morning I may have given him another Mars bar depending on how much work he had done.

At the lunch break I'd give the dog another Mars bar and then during the middle of the afternoon another one. This just about kept his sugar level right for the rest of the day.

At some pheasant shoots we do about four or five drives in the morning and about four drives in the afternoon. When my spaniel is working for the full day I give him about four large Mars bars throughout the day which keeps him working in top gear.

Most shooting men don't like to tell anybody if there is a fault with their gundog or dogs, because they all like to think that their dogs are perfect with no faults.

I know lots of shooting men with gundogs which have all sorts of faults. I have never come across a perfect gundog yet. Some gundog men will sometimes work one gundog in the morning at a pheasant shoot and then change the dog and have a new dog in the afternoon.

Other gundog men work the same dogs all day as I do and they also give their dogs a Mars bar or two during the day just to keep them going. Mars bars are nice to eat as well as being a quick source of sugar for both man and beast.

Not producing sufficient sugar is something new to me in dogs, but I can remember when I was a young boy sometimes one of our dairy cows would just stop eating.

It was normally a cow that was newly calved. When she was producing a lot of milk she couldn't produce enough sugar from her food intake to produce all this milk to feed her calf, and her body reaction was just to stop eating.

My father could tell you when a cow was going off her food, he could smell it in their breath. He used to play hell with us young boys because we couldn't tell when a cow was going off her food.

We used to give the sick cows a bottle of glucose straight into a blood vein in their neck. Sometimes a sick cow may need two or three bottles of glucose depending on how sick she was when we caught her.

After two or three days the sick cow would be eating again. There was a lot of milk lost as the cow's milk would quickly start to dry up when she wasn't eating any food. Some sick cows would never make up the lost milk during that lactation.

Both the cows and my spaniel dog were just the same, their bodies couldn't produce enough sugar when they were working at full stretch and they reacted in different ways. We just couldn't give the cows Mars bars!

My father was a very good stockman, he could soon tell us when a cow, calf, dog or horse was off colour just by looking at the animal's eyes and by smelling their breath. This was skill that none of us boys had, but he taught us a lot about animals.

Now let's get back to the law again. This is a story which I hope you enjoy. It was finally decided on by the courts and involved the Duke of Rutland in 1865.

When you travel out into the countryside and over the open moors you may wonder at times who owns them. Well they will either belong to some landowner, such as the Duke of Rutland, or some company such as the Water Board.

The Duke of Rutland owned some grouse moors and one day he was out shooting grouse with some friends. There was a public highway running between the Duke's moors and this person, who must have had a grudge against the Duke or his gamekeepers, thought he would stand on the public highway and try and prevent the grouse that were being driven towards the butts from crossing.

The Duke's gamekeepers approached this person and asked him to stop what he was trying to do and to move on. When he refused the gamekeepers held him down on the ground until the grouse drive was over.

This person then accused and reported the Duke and his gamekeepers for assault on the public highway and the matter ended up in court. The court held that the Duke had a vested interest in the soil under the public highway because he was the owner of the adjoining land on either side of the public highway.

This person was trying to use the public highway for a purpose other than that of passing and re-passing, he was thus a trespasser and the assault was justified.

There was another similar case which never came to the court, as *The Poacher's Lawyer* advised against it. There was a public footpath right through the middle of a pheasant wood, known as the Crow Wood, on this private estate.

One day the landowner was shooting pheasants from Crow Wood. As the gamekeepers and beaters were walking through the wood beating out the pheasants to the guns they came across this old and well known poacher called Darky. (Sounds like the name of a horse).

Darky was standing on the public footpath in the middle the wood with a dead pheasant in his hand. One of the gamekeepers asked Darky where he got the pheasant from. Darky said a farmer gave it to him and he was on his way home with it.

One of the two gamekeepers lunched at Darky and struck him a blow on the head, Darky fell back over onto the ground and as he was falling he dropped the pheasant.

The other gamekeeper quickly picked up the pheasant and found it had been recently shot and was still warm. Both gamekeepers then set about Darky and beat him up. The gamekeepers took the dead pheasant and left Darky lying on the public footpath in the middle of Crow Wood.

A few days later Darky went to see *The Poacher's Lawyer*. Darky sometimes left a brace of pheasants hanging on the office door for the lawyer. *The Poacher's Lawyer* knew Darky well and he knew he was a villain and quite a sly poacher.

When Darky entered the lawyer's office, *The Poacher's Lawyer* asked what he could do for him. Darky explained how he was beaten up by the two gamekeepers while he was on a public footpath in the middle of the wood where they were shooting pheasants and he would like to have them charged with assault.

The lawyer asked if it was in Crow Wood, which Darky confirmed. It took some time to get all the information out of Darky about the assault and the pheasant.

The Poacher's Lawyer then advised Darky to not take the matter any further and to not be in Crow Wood again when they were shooting pheasants, as the landowner had a vested interest in the soil under the public footpath there as his land adjoined the path.

Furthermore, as he was on the path in the wood to steal, he was trespassing in pursuit of game and the assault was justified.

The lawyer said good-bye to Darky and advised him not to do it again. As Darky was leaving the office, the lawyer said to him, 'And the next time that you are kind enough to leave a brace of pheasants hanging on the office door make sure they are shot birds and not birds with broken necks.'

Chapter 3   DUCKS & THE FORESHORE

There is a great charm in going after ducks, whether stalking them along the banks of a river or ditch, or waiting for them at flight time in the evening at a duck pond, or on the foreshore.

To enjoy the sport of duck shooting thoroughly they must be real wild ducks as they are one of the most alert birds and can be very difficult to attract into a pond or wet boggy area.

Rearing wild mallard ducks has now become a recognised branch of sport, as much as rearing pheasants or partridges, but it can sometimes be very difficult to train these hand reared ducks to fly.

Most hand reared ducks can be very difficult to flush from ponds, or lakes and sometimes you need a boat to get the ducks to lift from the water. When they do lift they will generally just circle round the pond, or lake, a few times then they just drop back down into the water.

At the turn of the last century, around 1904, Sir Richard Graham from Netherby Estate at Longtown in Cumberland, on the Scottish border, was the pioneer at rearing wild mallard ducks on ponds, which he had dug out on the estate.

He was very successful at rearing and shooting mallard ducks, as was shown by the following paragraph that appeared in the sporting press at the time.

A record bag of wild duck was made lately at Netherby Estate in Cumberland when Sir Richard Graham and a party of six guns shot 1,317 ducks in one day. These were hand reared mallard ducks flying from one pond to another on the estate.

The possibilities at the time, for hand rearing mallard ducks were great, but most sportsmen like wild ducks to shoot at because they offer a challenge in trying to bring the wild ducks in close enough to get a shot at them; if you can bag a few ducks it is even better still, but this day's duck shooting at Netherby was really outstanding.

We have lost many farm duck ponds in the last fifty years, as they have been filled in because of the changes in the agricultural industry.

This new industry, of rearing mallard ducks, has been aided by the many huge lakes that have been constructed in so many parts of the country to act as reservoirs in conserving a water supply for the large towns and cities.

These new reservoirs have increased largely the stock of wild mallard ducks in this country, as well as the many thousands of mallard ducks that are hand reared every year on shoots.

There are about forty different species of ducks and a great number of these ducks either breed in, or visit, the British Isles every year, but the mallard ducks are the most common ducks in this country. They can generally be found in lakes, ponds rivers and in other open watery, boggy places.

The male duck commonly known as the mallard is a beautiful bird. The head and upper part of the neck are a dark green, the lower part of the neck, which is separated from the upper part by a white ring, is a greyish brown colour.

The breast above is of a deep chestnut colour and below is a greyish white. The back is a greyish brown. The mallard wings which extend to nearly three feet are of a rich purple colour merging into black.

The male bird has a tail of twenty feathers, the four centre feathers are curled up and they are of a greenish black colour and the other tail feathers are greyish white.

The female is smaller than the male and is of a brown colour. The tail feathers are brown margined with a reddish white. The young ducks. both male and female, are known as flappers and resemble each other till after the first moult.

I have hand reared mallard ducks a number of times, on both farm ponds and wild ponds, but they were never as good to shoot at as the wild ducks were, as they never offered the variety of shots that wild ducks do. If you can get the hand reared ducks lifted off the pond into the air they will just circle around the pond not flying very fast, as they have lost the fear of man.

Hand reared ducks are an easy target to shoot at and they will sometimes fly round and round the pond until you have shot them all, as they are not even scared of the shots being fired.

Because hand reared ducks have lost the fear of man they can get nearly as tame as farm poultry and they don't offer the shooters very exciting sport. When a wild duck gets the sight of a human it takes off at a very high speed and within a few seconds it is half a mile up in the sky.

The money the 'townies' bring into the countryside helps to maintain some shoots and estates. It doesn't really matter whether or not they are any good at shooting, as long as plenty of game and wildfowl are flushed over them to see and they bring their money.

You can flush hand reared mallard ducks from one pond to another during the day, but you can't do this with wild ducks. It is only at about sunset that some of the best sport with wild ducks is obtained.

Wild duck will sometimes congregate at dusk in some pond or other where there is food and if the right place is found, the air will sometimes be thick with them flying to and fro. This period of flighting, as it is called, rarely lasts for more than half an hour.

My own shooting record I think is quite reasonable. In 1965 I shot 1,856 woodpigeons in two months and that was only shooting for a few hours during several days in each of the two months.

The woodpigeons were not hand reared, they were all wild and I shot most of them over decoys on wheat and barley fields. I probably shot a lot more woodpigeons than that, but that was what I collected.

I had some great fun shooting these woodpigeons, which were causing a lot of damage to the cereal crops. Some of the shots were quite easy, but other shots were very difficult and had me stretching. It was great sport in all weathers.

Now let me turn to the foreshore. What rights do you think you have to walk along the foreshore or even to shoot ducks on the foreshore; who does the foreshore actually belong to?

The sea and the shore have a great attraction to most people. The foreshore also attracts a number of people who like to shoot ducks and geese, but you just can't walk onto any foreshore to shoot wild ducks, as you may be trespassing to get there, as you have no more right to walk over your neighbour's land to get to the sea than to get to a public road.

For example if you want to get to a public road you either go across your own land, or land over which you have a private right of way, or by any other public road, and so it is with the sea.

The sea is public property on which all men can go and so is the foreshore proper, at least, even if this has been granted to a private person, the public still have rights of way over the foreshore.

A person, the Crown, or a company may own property and land right up to where the shore starts and they may also own part of the shore above the high water tide mark.

Below the high water tide mark and above the low water tide mark is where the public have a right of way at any time, but it is not always easy to get access to walk below the high water tide mark depending on the tides. When you walk on the foreshore above the high water tide mark you are very likely to be trespassing, as that land may belong to the Crown, to a company, or to a private person.

You have no right to go to the sea except where there is a public road leading down to it, not even if you want to go and wash yourself in the sea. Nor, can you claim a right to walk along the shore above the flow of the high tide.

That is the general law, although in some places it may be modified by an immemorial custom, for the inhabitants of a particular parish or district to exercise certain rights over the beach.

Many sportsmen go duck shooting on the foreshore. They will go well away out onto the shore when the tide is out 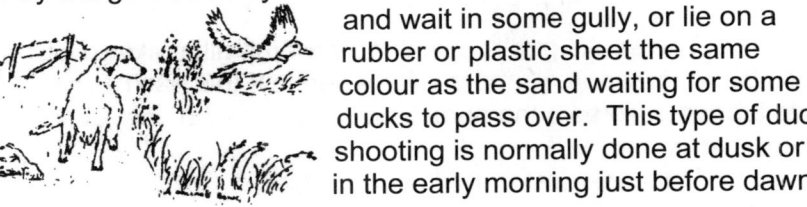 and wait in some gully, or lie on a rubber or plastic sheet the same colour as the sand waiting for some ducks to pass over. This type of duck shooting is normally done at dusk or in the early morning just before dawn.

Most duck shooters have permission to shoot on the foreshore. They may be a member of a club which has rented the duck shooting on part of the foreshore from the owner, or owners, of the foreshore.

These duck shooters may shoot ducks below the high water mark and above it and still be within the law, as they have permission to do so. The duck shooters may have to walk across the owner's land to get to the foreshore without knowing it.

There are two high tides remember. There is the normal high tide every day, then there is the spring high tide which usually comes further up the beach. The normal high tide mark would concern the general public most. Remember, if you happen to walk over and above the high water tide mark, you are almost sure to be walking on another man's land, or land belonging to the Crown.

Now let me tell you a story about a Mr Prowler who went duck shooting on the foreshore and ended up going to see *The Poacher's Lawyer* to get some advice on the matter.

Early on Monday November 14th 1901, from the small seaport town of Saltburn, Mr Prowler set off to walk along the beach with his shotgun and spaniel dog called Snip. He was going duck shooting further along the foreshore.

They had walked several miles along the beach when they came to some cliffs which jutted some considerable way out into the sea.

At the low water tide mark one could easily walk round the foot of the cliffs as there was quite a margin of beach between the cliffs; but at the half flood, the waves washed the cliffs and at the high water mark it was quite impossible to get round the cliffs unless you had a boat, or you were a good swimmer.

The cliffs were also unclimbable and the only other way to get to the cliffs was over private land. The public highway circled the cliffs some distance away. The general public tried to cut a permanent right of way for themselves by making a footpath along the cliffs.

The owner of the land and cliffs was a Lord Blake and he had a very difficult job trying to keep people and poachers off his land. He was hated by a lot of the local people, including Mr Prowler, for trying to stop them from crossing his land at the cliffs to get to the beach when the tide was in or out.

Lord Blake's gamekeepers had nearly a full time job chasing people from the land. Mr Prowler had rubbed shoulders with the gamekeepers on several occasions and was classed by them as being public enemy number one.

On the morning in question, when Mr Prowler reached the bottom of the cliffs, the tide had started to turn and Mr Prowler managed to wade round the cliffs before the water had actually left the face of the cliffs.

About a mile further along the foreshore Mr Prowler planted himself on the beach in an oilskin bag of similar colour to the beach. He lay there on the damp sand to ambush any wild ducks, which passed and re-passed from the sea to a private lake on Lord Blake's estate a short distance inland.

It was a rather boisterous morning and the sport was quite brisk as the ducks came to and fro from the sea to the lake. Mr Prowler was quite in order as he was shooting wild ducks below the high water tide mark. With all the banging going on the gamekeepers from Lord Blake's estate were soon down at the foreshore to see who was doing all the shooting. The gamekeepers kept above the high water level mark on their employer's land.

Mr Prowler was having some good sport among the wild ducks, although he wasn't hitting very many. As the day went on Mr Prowler moved back nearer to the shore as the light was fading. He then shot a duck which fell well above the high water level mark.

There was then a race for the dead duck between Mr Prowler, his dog Snip and the two gamekeepers. The dog got to the bird first, but one of the gamekeepers dived on the dog and took the duck from it. Snip then went for one of the gamekeepers while the other gamekeeper started beating Snip over the head with a big stick until the dog just dropped dead.

When Mr Prowler got to the gamekeepers he went for the one that he saw hitting Snip. In the scrimmage that followed between both gamekeepers and Mr Prowler, he ended up with two black eyes, a bruised skin and a very sore body. He also lost his duck and his dog

The excitement of the scrimmage between them had caused the time to slip by unheeded and Mr Prowler was reminded that he must get going or the in-coming tide would not only wash away his oilskin bag and his ducks, which lay on the sand, but would mean that he might also not get round the cliffs for the water.

Mr Prowler made a speedy retreat from the foreshore with his gun and ducks and he left his dead dog Snip lying on the beach above the high water level mark.

If Mr Prowler missed the tide and the water was too deep to get round the cliffs, it would mean either a ten mile walk along the beach to get to the public highway, or a mile walk over Lord Blake's land to get to the same highway.

Mr Prowler got back round the cliffs alright although he was feeling pretty annoyed with what the gamekeepers had done to him and his dog.

A few days, later with two black swollen eyes and very sore bones, Mr Prowler visited *The Poacher's Lawyer* to see if he could charge both gamekeepers with assault and for killing his dog.

When Mr Prowler met *The Poacher's Lawyer* he burst out, 'I was shooting ducks on the foreshore where any of His Majesty's subjects has a right to be and to shoot ducks, too, unless I am very much mistaken, in law.'

The Poacher's Lawyer said, 'That all depends on to whom the foreshore belongs. Presumably it belongs to the crown or, as we lawyers always say, in law to the (*prima facie*) and all the public have rights of passage over, it just as they have over public roads.'

The lawyer also said, 'Maybe Lord Blake has in his possession a grant from the Crown to himself or to a predecessor in title for this particular piece of foreshore, above the high water tide mark, if so the shooting will belong to him. However, even if the foreshore does belong to Lord Blake because he has adjoining land, and in fact it is more likely to belong to him than anyone else except to the Crown, you still have the right of passage over the foreshore below the high water tide mark, which no Grant from the Crown can take away from you.'

The lawyer continued, 'As you shot the ducks below the high water level mark, the ducks belong to you, even those that fell above the high water level mark; but you have no right to go onto Lord Blake's land to pick them up as you would then be trespassing.'

'Your proper course of action, Mr Prowler, would have been to have respectfully asked for your ducks from the gamekeepers and if the gamekeepers refused to deliver them, well perhaps then you might have brought an action against Lord Blake.'

Mr Prowler then said, 'Do you mean to say that I have no right, as one of the public, to go onto the foreshore when the tide is in? For that is what it amounts to, if I must not walk above the ordinary high water mark, how can I then get down to the sea?'

The lawyer said, 'As I have explained to you the sea is public property, but you only have a right to go to the sea where there is a public road leading down to it. As far as the beating the gamekeepers gave you, they had every right as you attacked one of them for hitting your dog while you were trespassing on Lord Blake's land. As far as your dog Snip is concerned the gamekeepers had no right to kill your dog simply because it was trespassing, nor because it had taken up a duck you had no right to get. Didn't you say, Mr Prowler, that Snip attacked one of the gamekeepers?'

Mr Prowler replied, 'Well it flew at his leg when he tried to take the duck from it, and he, in self protection, hit my dog across the head with a stick.'

The lawyer said, 'I know a spaniel can give you a nasty bite, though I don't intend to insinuate that it was necessary to kill the dog. However the gamekeeper was clearly justified in giving the dog a sufficiently hard blow to send it about its business and if by mistake in his agitation he hit it a little too hard, or struck it in a more vital spot than he intended, well the dog's death might have been unintentional after all. You take my meaning, Mr Prowler?'

Mr Prowler said, 'You mean to say, Sir, I suppose, that the gamekeepers would swear that the dog attacked one of them savagely and the other gamekeeper only hit the dog hard enough to drive it off, but somehow, quite unbeknown to them the dog got killed?'

'Precisely,' said the lawyer to Mr Prowler, 'and I think the very best thing you can do is to pocket your pride and try and

forget all about the unpleasant scrimmage between yourself and Lord Blake's gamekeepers. Good-bye, Mr Prowler, good-bye.'

Now let me tell you about the two duck ponds which I have. They are both flighting ponds and give me and my friends about twenty minutes to half an hour's duck shooting at dusk. Its wonderful sport while it lasts.

Both ponds are fenced off and the bigger of the two ponds is near to a large city, it measures about fifty yards long by twenty yards wide and has a row of hardwood trees along each side of the pond.

I don't have any duck hides at this pond. When I go to this pond for duck shooting I normally invite another two or three shooters with me and we all sit along one side of the pond. So all the guns are shooting either across the pond or up into the sky.

Nobody is allowed to shoot down into the pond while the ducks are flighting, just in case one of the shooters' dogs has jumped into the pond and is going after a duck that has been shot and is lying in the water. This is for safety reasons and to see that a dog doesn't get shot.

Because this pond is long, with trees on either side of it, the ducks always seem to come in from one end of the pond no matter what the weather is like and the gun sitting at that end of the pond gets the first shot at the ducks.

After the first shot is fired the ducks either break and double back out of the pond or they fly right along the middle the other guns a shot at them. It's great fun and great sport.

When the ducks are flying along this pond they are normally always rising and flying very fast and the shooters don't have much time to get a shot at them because of the tree branches. You have to be wide awake and ready for the ducks which can be a tremendous challenge just to get a shot at them. This is what the sport is all about and not about how many ducks you shoot.

I am well aware that wild ducks normally drop into a pond against the wind, but in this long pond which faces east-west, the oak and beech trees are so high that the ducks seem to favour dropping into the pond at one end. When the ducks drop underneath the top of the trees the wind direction is broken anyway.

I feed the wild ducks with barley once or twice a week, mainly at the other end of the pond to where they come in, because its easier to feed the ducks at that end of the pond and the ducks soon swim along to the feed.

The other duck pond which I have is much smaller, but it is also a very useful pond and is a lovely pond. It is fairly open and is more in the country and faces east to west. There are some nice shrubs around this pond which helps to break up the bareness and makes it very private.

This is also a flighting pond and the ducks come to and fro for about half an hour at dusk. I have built three wooden hides along one side and they are built like grouse butts. I have plastic crates in the hides for the shooters to sit on.

Also, on each of the wooden duck hides I have sticks or goal posts, sticking up on each side. This is to stop the guns from swinging round and shooting the person in the other butts.

I am very conscious of the safety factor when I am out shooting in the field, as I think there are far too many careless shooting accidents caused by shooters not thinking and not taking enough care.

The mallard ducks coming to this pond normally circle the pond a few times before they drop into the feed. As the pond is more open the ducks drop into it against the wind.

I normally have a gun in each hide and if they have dogs with them the dogs sit in the hides with the shooters and then at the end of the flighting, we all pick up or hunt for any ducks that have been shot. This pond also provides some good sport and good fun.

I feed the ducks at this pond with either barley or wheat, which ever I can get hold of and which ever is the cheapest. I mainly feed barley and feed the ducks twice a week and have a shoot about once a fortnight or so.

We normally shoot a few ducks depending a great deal on the weather. With duck shooting you can never guarantee that the ducks will come into the pond. But there are not many nights that we don't at least get one or two.

I have been asked a number of times if wild ducks can smell. Well they appear to have a very keen

THE HAUNT OF SNIPE

scent indeed. When stalking ducks sitting out in the middle of a river and a detour has to be made in order to approach them and get a shot at them, it is necessary to be very careful about crossing the wind for if it is blowing towards the ducks they will instantly pick up the scent and rise when the shooter is a long way off although the ducks cannot see or hear him.

Shooting flighting ducks at dusk is not as easy as it seems. The ducks coming into the pond are usually so close before they can be seen at night that little allowance need be made in front of the birds as nearly all misses occur from aiming too low.

When the light is bad there is a strong tendency for duck shooters to lower the muzzle of the gun in order to try and see the ducks, so they shoot underneath the birds. It is better to aim rather higher when the birds are rising.

Chapter 4   THE SPORTSMAN & HIS DOG

We are a nation of animal lovers, especially of dogs. Many game shooters and gamekeepers keep dogs of a variety of breeds for working among game. Dogs are part of the tools of the trade in country sports.

I have often heard it said when I am out shooting with my gundogs. How on earth can some people go shooting without a gundog? However, I quite understand why some shooters don't keep a dog.

They may not have the time to look after a dog, or they may not have the house or garden to properly keep a dog in. Dogs soon get bored if they have nothing to do and are shut up in a house all day. They will soon find some mischief to get up to.

Many shooters would love to have a gundog, when they are out shooting and they would be willing to pay a lot of money for a good gundog, but this is not to be with some shooters and they often tell me, when they see me working my dogs at some shoots, that they would love to have a dog like mine.

Dogs take a lot of work and attention to look after and you have to be prepared to give up quite a lot of your time to look after them properly. If you happen to have gundogs and you work them in the field, then you also have all the bangs and knocks to attend to that they get when they are out working in the field.

I have kept gundogs all my life of various breeds and have had good dogs and even better dogs, but I have never owned a dog that's been perfect. Dogs, like humans, have all got faults of some sort or another.

I have many tales which I can tell you about working dogs over the years, and will tell you a few stories about dogs throughout the book which have burned their way into my memory.

My main aim in this chapter is to look at and discuss some of the liabilities which attach themselves to the ownership of dogs, mainly from a sportsman's point of view.

To sum up, at the beginning, so long as our dog behaves himself as properly brought up dogs should, then we are under no liability to anyone. For the simple reason that properly behaved dogs never injure anyone.

But to go a bit further than this, if your dog usually behaves in a well bred manner then you are not to be held liable if the dog forgets once in a while and gives way to sudden impulses and causes some damage.

To take a simple instance, if you enter another man's land without his permission and without any legal right, you are guilty of a common law trespass and are liable to an action, for at least nominal damages, and if you do any actual damage you render yourself liable to the more summary remedy of a summons before the magistrates for malicious damage.

If, however, you are walking along a road with your dog and the dog is a well-behaved one, you are not liable for any little excursion he may take on his own account if he jumps into a neighbour's land and causes some damage.

For example, in a case that went before the Courts, a Labrador dog owned by a Mr A was taken for a walk by a friend Mr B. On returning to A's house the dog suddenly took it into his head to make an exhibition of his jumping powers and leaped the wooden fence into a garden adjoining his master's.

Unfortunately the dog landed on the back of the neighbour, who was digging his garden, and he was seriously injured.

The neighbour brought an action against the dog's owner Mr A and against Mr B as the person in charge of the dog, but it was held at Court that the neighbour could not recover anything, as the dog jumped the fence without the will or any consent of his master, or Mr B. Meaning that the dog wasn't sent to jump over the neighbour's fence.

There is an old saying that every dog is entitled to one bite, which is not literally correct, but contains a great many grains of truth.

If, however, the owner of a dog incites or encourages his dog to do damage or even to enter another man's land, it is a

very different story. For in this case he is liable to make good any damage that is caused by the dog.

If no visible damage is committed, the occupier of the property into which the dog trespasses would still have the right to recover nominal damages in a civil action, if he though it worth his while to bring one, as it would be very difficult to prove in Court.

I must tell you this story about a collie dog we had on the farm, which I will take to my grave with me. The dog was called Bess and she was born on the farm. She was a lovely natured dog and never had an ounce of bad in her.

Bess used to follow my father all over the farm, anywhere he went she was at his heels. We had too many collie dogs on the farm at the time and one day at the cattle market my father sold Bess to a farmer away down on the west coast of Scotland at Stranraer, about forty odd miles away.

Bess was just over a year old at the time and my father sold her for £40 on a six months trial period. She was from good stock and was shaping into being a useful dog among either sheep or cattle.

The following Sunday morning the farmer and his wife from Stranraer arrived at the farm to collect Bess. We were all very sad to see her go. My father said we had plenty of collie dogs and she was going to a good home to work amongst both sheep and cattle.

Several weeks had passed by and then one morning the farmer from Stranraer phoned my father to tell him that Bess was missing and had been missing for two days. Don't worry, said my father, she will turn up as she is a very friendly dog.

Sadly, a few days later the farmer from Stranraer phoned again and told my father that Bess was still missing. My father asked the farmer to look in his farm outbuildings as she might be hiding in one of them.

Then one very wet Wednesday morning when we got up my father was first out the farm back door and there Bess was, lying at the door in a terrible state. She was wet, very thin and her paws were red raw and some were bleeding.

My father lifted Bess up and brought her into the warmth of the back kitchen. The whole family were round the dog like bees round a hive, including myself.

What a super dog Bess was, she had walked back home from Stranraer, some forty odd miles away. How she found her way home we will never know, as she had never been away from home before.

Bess fully recovered after a few weeks and my father could not bring himself to part with her again. He sent the Stranraer farmer back his £40 and Bess, who followed my father everywhere, was treated by him and the rest of the family like a queen till she died some fifteen years later.

When Bess died it was like losing a member of the family. We were all devastated by her death and my father decided to bury her in the rose garden in front of the farm house, where she still lies today.

Now let me tell you about what the courts had to say about a dog which was set off, or incited, to chase a hare and another well behaved dog which was so excited, (by the other dog chasing after the hare), that it broke and joined in the chase, which ended up with the dogs causing a lot of damage resulting in the case being brought to Court.

The Poacher's Lawyer was a witness to this case with the dogs so he had first hand knowledge of what actually happened.

His Honour the Judge took the word of *The Poacher's Lawyer* as being the true facts of the case before making his decision. This is what happened.

One day *The Poacher's Lawyer* was out with a small shooting party, it was a very small party for there were only the host, a farmer whom I will call Mr A, the lawyer and a clerk and a young friend whom I will call young Mr Z.

They had two dogs with them at the shoot. Mr A, the farmer, had a Labrador with him and young Mr Z had a springer spaniel. They were both well trained, obedient dogs and had never caused any trouble before.

The party spent the morning walking up pheasant, partridge, hares and rabbits and at mid day they sat down to a well earned lunch. The spot they had selected to have their lunch was, unfortunately, at the end of a field adjoining a neighbouring farmer who had sheep in the field.

While they were busy engaged in looking after the inner man, a hare ran across the field in the direction of the neighbour's land. There was no time for any of the party to pick up a gun and have a shot at the hare, but the young friend Mr Z, with his lack of experience sent his spaniel after the hare as it neared the boundary fence.

THE SMOOTH FOX-TERRIER

'After him Jack, good dog find him, find him,' called out young Mr Z. This was too much for Mr A's Labrador which also set off in pursuit of the hare. Mr A, the farmer, was furious and he called young Mr Z all the names under the sun for such a stupid action.

In vain, the farmer tried to whistle his dog back, but the dog took no notice of its master's voice or whistle, and so both dogs were soon running across the next field, among the neighbour's sheep.

In due time the dogs returned very much exhausted and looking rather ashamed of themselves. Unfortunately, the neighbouring farmer was expecting some early lambs to arrive in a fortnight's time, but ten ewes had their lambs later that day and eight of the ten lambs died that night. The sheep farmer was naturally very annoyed and made a claim against Mr A for damages. Mr A thought the amount the sheep farmer was claiming was extortionate and although he didn't want his neighbour to suffer any loss, he offered him half what he was asking.

This was refused and the sheep farmer then brought an action in the County Court against Mr A and young Mr Z as the owners of the dogs.

The Poacher's Lawyer and his clerk were summoned as witnesses on behalf of the sheep farmer. *The Poacher's Lawyer* knew the judge and on examination and cross examination, the lawyer stated the facts as to how the dogs had started to chase the hare.

The judge accepted the lawyer's statement that both dogs were well trained and invariably well behaved and obedient to their masters' commands.

Young Mr Z, in a moment of thoughtlessness, had sent his dog after the hare; whilst Mr A's dog just took off in the excitement. Mr A had at once tried to recall his dog.

The Poacher's Lawyer was asked if young Mr Z had not sent his dog after the hare would Mr A's dog have pursued the hare? 'No,' said the lawyer, 'he would not have chased after the hare on his own under his master's eyes.'

This was the decision of the judge and the Court. His Honour the judge did not require to hear the defendants themselves as he accepted the evidence of the lawyer to be correct.

The judge merely called for some expert evidence to prove that the amount claimed for damages was excessive. At the conclusion of the case the judge without hesitation gave judgement to the sheep farmer against young Mr Z, but dismissed the action against Mr A.

It was a satisfactory outcome for Mr A, because the damages awarded to the sheep farmer had to be paid for by young Mr Z and the amount was slightly less than the amount Mr A had originally offered his neighbour.

I have explained what the law is when a dog is sent or is incited by its master to make a chase. As a rule, where the dog has not been sent to make a chase, there is no liability on the dog's owner.

The exception to this is where a dog owner knows his dog will chase a hare if it gets a chance and causes damage. To make the dog owner liable there must be this knowledge known to lawyers as *scienter* on the part of the owner. This is the origin of the old saying that a dog is entitled to one bite.

It does not matter what the particular vice or mischief the dog does. The owner is liable if he knows his dog causes damage to other people, or their property, and he does nothing about it.

Most shoot owners near towns and cities are sometimes troubled with stray dogs chasing and killing some young pheasant poults. The question here arises, can the shoot owner substantiate a claim against the dog owner? Was the dog known to chase and kill young pheasants and did the dog owner know this? If the answer is yes, then the dog owner is liable to pay for all the damage done by his dog.

If the answer is no, then the dog owner is under no liability at all and it lies on the person, whose pheasants were killed, to prove otherwise.

The law is precisely the same in the case of a dog biting anyone. The person bitten must prove to the Court that the owner knew the dog was dangerous and would bite people.

However, a law created by an Act of 1867 states that if a dog bites or worries sheep, cattle or horses then it shall not be necessary to prove *scienter*, or to know on part of the dog owner. For the dog owner is liable for all the damage as a matter of course.

It is, as we all know, a common practice for some sportsmen and gamekeepers to shoot dogs and cats seen in the woods or anywhere near to where they are rearing game birds. The shooter very rarely thinks to inquire whether such shooting is justifiable.

The law is quite clear on this matter and states that no one can justify shooting or killing a trespassing dog, merely because it is trespassing, nor can they justify shooting or killing a dog that has been destroying some of their game birds.

This was settled in 1809 in a Court case, which went even further in deciding that the mere proof that the dog was running after a hare was no excuse for a gamekeeper to shoot the dog.

In that case Lord Ellenborough said, 'A dog does not incur the penalty of death for running after a hare on another man's land, and anyone that disagrees with that reason and the common sense, is in no authority to govern other cases.'

However the act of killing a dog may be justified, if it can be shown that the dog was chasing, or in the act of killing, preserved game, and that it was necessary to kill the dog in order to save the game. Golden pheasants, pheasants, partridge and guinea fowl all come under 'preserved game'.

How often this could be proved would be extremely difficult to say, for, of the number of dogs that are shot by gamekeepers and sportsmen, only the very odd ones are killed under circumstances that the law would consider justifiable.

The same rules apply to cats. You can always frighten a cat that has not actually seized the game, although shouting or the like might not sometimes have the same effect on a dog.

The only case in which the shooting of a cat could be excused on the grounds of necessity, is where the cat is running away with, say, a poult in its mouth and the shooter kills the cat and not the poult and the poult's life is actually saved.

The owner of a shoot or his gamekeeper has no more legal right to seize, or shoot, the dog of a poacher, which he surprises on a poaching expedition, than he has to take a dog that has strayed on to his land without its owner's knowledge.

One exception to this rule is created by the Game Act of 1831, which empowers the lord of a manor, lordship or royalty to authorise his gamekeeper, under his hand and seal, to seize dogs that are being used for taking the lord's game within the limits of the manor.

This is of minor importance, but it is still the law today and the lords and landowners still have a great deal of power in this country.

The general rule of law appears to be that no man may justify killing a dog or cat in defence of his game, unless he can show that, but for his killing the dog, the game would have been killed and that there was no other way of saving it. If a dog is worrying sheep and is caught red handed you can shoot it.

Let me now tell you about a dog I had, a springer spaniel. I said previously that I have never had a perfect dog before, well this dog was getting on that way, he was a brilliant dog at his work in the field among game.

This dog was called Patch, he was well marked and came from a good working strain of spaniel dogs. I got him as a puppy at ten weeks old and more or less started training him straight away. At the time I bought Patch, I was doing a lot of shooting of all sorts, pheasants, grouse, ducks, partridge, rabbits and woodpigeons.

When Patch was fifteen months old he was with me at all types of shooting, and I just kept training and training the young dog. Little did I know at the time that Patch was learning his craft well and would turn out to be the best dog I ever had, with regards to being a working, intelligent dog.

If there was a bush lying ahead of us when Patch was working in the field he could tell me if there were any game birds in the bush. Well before we ever got to it, he had the bush covered with his nose.

Many times I was walking up pheasants with some friends and my dog Patch. The dog would sometimes just dash past a bush which was a likely spot to hold game birds. A friend might say to me to put the dog in the bush. I would reply that there is nothing in the bush or the dog would have been in after it.

But just to convince my friend that I was right, I would call Patch up and send him into the bush. Sure enough there would be nothing in the bush. I never knew the dog to be wrong.

Patch was so clever at his craft and work that at times he used to think ahead of me. It took me sometime to catch up with what the dog was up to, but once I saw how clever he was, we had a great working relationship together.

For instance, if some shooters with their dogs were hunting for a shot bird, that was supposed to have dropped into a scrub area, and the person that shot the bird was pretty sure the bird was dead, if Patch and I joined in the hunt, and if my dog didn't show any interest within a few minutes, I knew there was nothing there and would say so.

This was a dog that I could put into one end of a small covert and I would go to the far end of the covert and the dog would work the covert through to me, he was that good.

Some shooters used to think I was being rude, when the dogs were hunting for a supposed fallen bird and I just called my dog up and stopped him wasting his time. I was always right, or what I should say, is my dog Patch was always right.

If I asked Patch to track down a wounded bird and the bird was on the ground no matter how far it had travelled the dog would return with it. I once watched Patch crossing a small stream while tracking down a wounded cock pheasant which he returned with.

I really never appreciated how good this dog was until I didn't have him. I had another spaniel at the time and he was also a dog and was pretty useful in many ways which Patch had taught him, but he could never think ahead the way Patch used to do.

Patch was nine years old when I sadly had to put him to sleep. He was just in his prime and was a dog who was a pleasure to take anywhere. What happened to him was just one of those things that happens when you have working gundogs.

One day at a pheasant shoot Patch, like always, was working well. We had just finished a drive and were walking to the last drive before lunch when we came to this stone wall, there are a lot of stone walls in the north.

The wall was on a hillside and was under two metres from the top side, but the dog and I approached the wall from the low side so it was over two metres high.

I had climbed over the wall and turned round and noticed the dog was trying hard to climb up and get over the wall top. The dog had two or three goes at trying to get up and over the wall by himself, until I pulled him up and over.

What I didn't know at the time was the dog had pulled or strained his heart, when he was trying so hard to get up over the wall top. I noticed as we walked to the next pheasant drive that the dog wasn't well, something was very wrong with him.

We had just started the pheasant drive before lunch. Patch was at my heel at the time, then I just happened to turn round and there he was lying on his side as if he was exhausted.

I took him home after this and had him checked over with the Vet. Two Vets examined the dog and they were pretty sure he had strained his heart.

I tried all sorts of treatments and pills to get Patch sorted out after this, but I was fighting a losing battle with him. One of the side effects of the treatment was that fluid kept building up behind his heart which caused all sorts of problems, mainly him being sick at any time anywhere.

At the end of the day it was much kinder to have Patch put to sleep than to let him struggle on with all the problems he had. This was a dog which I will always remember, for the many good hunting days we had together.

Now let us look at the law on dog spears. Mr A was walking with his dog along a footpath in Mr B's field. A rabbit ran across the footpath and the dog started after it.

As the dog was going into a wood after the rabbit it ran onto a dog spear and was killed. Mr A then sued Mr B. Although it was admitted that Mr B set the spear for the purpose of killing dogs in pursuit of game, it was decided by the Court that Mr B was not liable.

It is the rule of law, that when a person or an animal is trespassing they take the risk of the pitfalls they find on the property, except where the owner is absolutely forbidden to erect spears.

But why a man should be permitted to place spears in a wood for the purpose of killing trespassing dogs, when he could use his gun for the same purpose, is one of the mysteries of the law which *The Poacher's Lawyer* has been unable to fully explain.

A man can also set traps for dogs (or cats) and he may bait them with as strongly a scented meat that he likes, but the baits must not be so near the highway, or his neighbour's land, that they can be scented beyond his boundary.

He is not entitled to tempt dogs to their doom from outside his own fence. If he does, he is liable to pay damages to the owner of the animal killed or injured.

It is also illegal to lay poisoned meat on land except in an enclosed garden (Poisoned Flesh Prohibition Act 1864). The person laying poisoned flesh is also liable to a civil action in respect of any dog or cat so killed.

A HEAD OF CORN

Chapter 5

CAN ANYONE SHOOT GROUND GAME WITHOUT A LICENCE?

The above title is quite easy to understand, but what does it really mean and can anyone shoot ground game without a licence? First of all ground game means Hares and Rabbits only.

There is a section in the Ground Game Act of 1880 and this is what it says. *The occupier and the person duly authorised by him shall not be required to obtain a licence to kill ground game on land he occupies.* Speaking mainly from a tenant farmer's point of view.

In that same section there is also a mention of the Gun Licence Act of 1870, which states that no persons are exempt from the provisions of the Gun Licence Act of 1870. Which means that if you own a shotgun legally, then you should have a licence for it.

The difference between a gun licence and a game licence is you need a gun licence before you can buy a shotgun and you need a game licence before you can shoot game.

So is it really necessary for a tenant farmer to have a gun licence to shoot hares and rabbits on land he occupies? The answer to this question is Yes. In the Gun Licence Act of 1870 section 3, it states he also needs a game licence to shoot hares, and *after the first day of April 1870 there shall be granted and paid unto, for the use of Her Majesty, her heirs and successors, a licence shall be taken out yearly by every person who shall use or carry a gun in the United Kingdom, the sum of ten shillings* - which is 50 pence today.

In this Act the term 'gun' includes a firearm of any description, an air-gun, or any other kind of gun from which any shot bullet or other missile can be discharged. This definition would appear to include a cross-bow.

These Acts of Parliament I have quoted all talk about a licence to kill game, certificates and a game licence. If for instance you go on to a public common, where you only have a right to walk about, and you shoot a rabbit, do you need a game licence for this?

Let me just refer back to the 1860 Act. This Act was passed to replace duties on game certificates, duties on excise licences and certificates.

Section 4 of the 1860 Act states: *That every person before he shall in Great Britain take, kill or pursue any game or any woodcock, snipe, quail or landrail and use any dog, gun or nets to pursue the game shall take out a proper licence to kill game under the Act.*

First of all you will need a gun certificate to own a gun, I am talking about a shotgun, and you will need a firearm certificate, if you want to own a rifle today.

The second point is you shouldn't be walking about on a public common with a loaded gun in pursuit of game, as you are trespassing and can be prosecuted for it and your gun could be taken from you.

The gist of the Acts you have read so far, more or less, means that prior to the 1860 Act, owners and occupiers of land didn't need a licence to kill ground game on their land. Remember, today you need a shotgun certificate to own a shotgun, and you need a game licence to shoot game, which you renew each year.

A game licence can be taken out from the 1st of August each year and it costs £6. This is to cover grouse shooting, but if you don't shoot grouse you can take a game licence out on the 1st of November and this costs £4. Both dates run to the end of July the following year.

The Game and Trespass Acts are slightly different in Ireland, Scotland and England, although a number of the Acts are relevant to the whole of the United Kingdom.

For instance, in Ireland, trespassing in pursuit of game in the daylight is prohibited by the Game Trespass Act, which was passed in 1864.

In Scotland the Act is the Day Trespass Act, officially called the Game (Scotland) Act, of 1832. This Act imposes a penalty on anyone who trespasses on any land in the daytime in pursuit of game, or of deer, roe, woodcock, snipes, quails, landrails, wild ducks or rabbits. The penalty is larger if the offender has his face blackened or is otherwise disguised (Wonderful!).

In England the law on day poaching is contained in the Game Act of 1831. By this Act a penalty is imposed on anyone who trespasses in the daytime on any land in pursuit of game, or woodcock, snipes, quail, landrails or rabbits. The penalty is increased if five or more persons trespass together.

In England and Ireland it is illegal to kill game on Sunday

or Christmas Day. There is no such direct prohibition in Scotland, but the Act of 1661, which is still in force today in Scotland, prohibits salmon fishing on the Sabbath Day. Under this Act a conviction for shooting on Sunday might be obtained.

It's a bit heavy going, beavering through the Acts. So let me now have a whisky, or two, before I tell you two stories about my father and his gundogs. I like a malt whisky or two. My

father used to say there wasn't such a thing as bad whisky, there was only good whisky and better whisky.

I will continue with the Ground Game Act of 1880 after I tell you these two stories about my father and his gundogs. He loved his shooting and his gundogs, which he bred himself.

My father mainly bred Spaniels and Labradors, but he did, however, keep the odd terrier or two from time to time and we always had two or three farm collie dogs running around.

He always had at least four gundogs at any one time. My father could really handle dogs, even the most difficult dogs could be brought to his heel. He used to train and treat all the injuries which his dogs got when they were working out in the field.

The gundogs were part of my father's tools of his trade. He had this large, rough shoot which held a great variety of game and wildfowl. There was also a very long large plantation in the shoot, where my father reared a few pheasants every year for shooting.

It was a great shoot, for working gundogs on, as there was plenty of cover. My father used to invite some friends over for a day's shooting about once a fortnight. It was mainly walking up game with gundogs. I used to walk in between the guns as a beater and I carried my father's game bag and any game he had shot.

There were normally about six or seven guns at the shoots, and we all finished up in the farmhouse having a meal, and some drinks, which my mother had prepared.

The tractor and trailer were used to take the guns around the shoot. We had a few bales of hay or straw lying on the trailer for the shooters to sit on. But it was open to the elements.

The rain never seemed to bother the shooters very much, but if there was a strong wind and it caught the tails of the pheasants and partridge when they were flushed, they would swing and swerve in the wind, and they could be very difficult to shoot. What wonderful sport.

One day my father was out with a shooting party. He had two Labrador dogs with him that day, a dog called Bob and a bitch called Sheila. I, as usual, was there doing all the humping and carrying for the guns.

The guns were walking in line near the edge of the far side of the shoot. My father was working his two dogs Bob and Sheila, when Sheila flushed a cock pheasant near the boundary, which my father shot and it fell on the other side of the fence.

My father sent Sheila to pick up the dead bird from over the boundary fence which was partly a thorn hedge, with a few strands of barbed wire running through it.

As Sheila jumped through the fence to go and retrieve the dead pheasant, she caught her belly on a loose bit of barbed wire, which tore a deep gash.

When Sheila returned with the pheasant she was covered in blood. When my father examined her the gash in her belly was about six inches long. My father blew the whistle to stop the line of guns. He called me over with his game bag, which also had a small leather bag in the back.

What happened next really amazed me as well as all the other shooters. My father simply opened his game bag and took out a thin rope muzzle, which he made himself and placed it over Sheila's head. The muzzle was tied fairly tight around the dog's neck.

He then took out a needle, which was already threaded with fishing line. He also took out his hip flask, which contained good malt whisky. He then turned Sheila over on her back and he asked me to hold the dog's front legs and to hold her head down.

My father then quickly poured some whisky from his flask over the dog's wound. Sheila didn't like it very much, as she let out a yelp or two, when the whisky stung the open wound.

He then started to stitch up the dog's wound with the needle and thread. Everybody just stood and stared with their mouths open, including myself, as he efficiently stitched up the dog. Within two or three minutes the job was done.

Sheila was then lifted and carried onto the tractor's trailer. She was left sitting on the trailer between the straw bales till the

shooters returned to the farm for their lunch.

The chat over lunch was all about how quickly my father had dealt with the dog's injuries. I had seen him inject dogs before and trim their claws and give them medicine, but I had never before seen him stitching up a dog's wounds.

Sheila recovered in about ten days and she was then out working in the field again. Sheila was a good working dog, but she had a bit of a temper and would think nothing of giving you a short sharp nip, if you pressed too close into her private life.

I was amazed at how good and quick my father was at stitching up the dog. Following this incident I saw him a number of times after that, stitching up a dog's torn ear and dogs with torn limbs. When guests were invited to shoot with my father they knew that if anything happened to their dogs my father would attend to them.

My father was never trained how to stitch up dogs that were wounded in the field, he just did it automatically and he became very efficient at it. He soon made a name for himself for treating dogs. Many gundog men that were invited to our shoots thought my father was as good, if not better, than many of the vets at treating dogs.

The other story I thought would interest you about my father and a gundog was on a day we were out on the moor shooting grouse. We were walking up the grouse and shooting them over dogs.

A guest and friend of my father had this big black Labrador dog called Tam with him that day. He was a vicious bad, tempered dog and would fight with any dogs that went near him. No matter what their sex was Tam would have a go at them.

The owner of Tam had some control over him, but it was up to the other dog owners to keep their dogs away from Tam for they knew he would have a go at them.

When Tam started working the moor flushing grouse he forgot all about fighting and worked away like a champion among the other dogs. It was only when he was idle that he became a bit vicious.

Tam was a big strong dog and he had teeth on him like a lion. I had seen him attack a much smaller dog than himself and the smaller dog would be finished and not work for the rest of the day. This caused a bit of trouble between Tam's owner and some of the other gundog owners.

This particular day, however, I was walking on the moor between my father with his two dogs and Tam's owner walking up grouse. There were seven guns out this day and two gamekeepers who were flushing the grouse with their dogs.

We were all walking up to this plain wire fence which parted the two moors. There were four or five strands of plain wire on the fence and some of the wire was loose and was twisted around some of the other strands of wire.

As we were all getting nearer to the wire fence the dogs were working out in front of the guns some twenty five yards Tam and the other dogs were working at full stretch.

When Tam came to the wire fence he tried to jump through it and push on, but one of his front legs caught the loose wires and as he was going through the fence the loose wires twisted and trapped his leg.

The twisted wires pulled Tam right over on his back and he started yelping with the pain of his leg being trapped in the wires.

The more Tam pulled his leg the more the pain increased and the more Tam kept yelping and yelping. We could see the dog was very distressed and was suffering considerable pain.

One of the gamekeepers who was nearest to Tam dashed forward to help him. My father called at the gamekeeper to leave the dog, as he would bite his head off.

Within a few minutes there were a few shooters and myself around Tam. He was struggling to free himself as he kept yelping and yelping at the top of his voice.

My father stepped forward and told the other guests to just stand back, or the trapped dog would bite them. My father then simple took off his woollen scarf and folded the scarf until it was about the size of a small rabbit.

He them walked over to Tam who snarled at him. My father then pushed the scarf into the dog's mouth and the dog sunk his teeth into the scarf. While Tam was biting hard on the scarf, my father released the dog's leg from the wire.

This was so simply done and the panic was over. Tam was none the worse for his ordeal and started working again

straight away. So a little tip for all you gundog lovers, if your dog gets trapped or even injured, think first, don't just dive in there to help your dog or you are likely to get bitten.

Shove something into the dog's mouth first, such as your cap, a glove, a bit of wood, or your scarf, before you tempt to free a trapped dog, especially if the dog is suffering some pain. The nicest of dogs can change when they are in pain.

When a landowner lets a farm to a tenant and he reserves the game rights, he becomes liable for damages, if the tenant's crop is damaged by the game.

The Ground Game Act of 1880 was passed to enable farm tenants as the occupiers of the land, to protect their crops from injury and loss by ground game. As I have mentioned previously ground game means hares and rabbits.

The Act gives the occupier (farm tenant) a right to shoot rabbits on his farm if they are eating his crops.

There is no definition of an occupier, but it will mainly be farm tenants. However section 1 of the Act tells us what persons are not to be deemed occupiers of land.

They are persons having a right of common only, and persons having a right of grazing or pasturage for sheep, cattle, or horses for not more than nine months in any year.

So as is common, in some districts, a person takes grassland from the early summer to Michaelmas, at the end of September, or to November. The game and rabbits will belong to the landlord, as the hirer has no right to the ground game under the Act.

The conditions under the Act over which the occupier of the land can exercise his right may be summarised as follows.

(1) The occupier can exercise the right himself, or through persons duly authorised by him in writing, but such persons must be either a member of his *household* resident on the land, or persons in his *ordinary service* working on the land, or *one person bona fide employed for reward* (being paid for killing and taking ground game on his land).

(2) Only the occupier himself and one other person (who must come under one of the classes above mentioned) can kill ground game with firearms.

(3) Any person authorised as above must be prepared at any time to produce his written authority on demand, and must produce it to the person who has the shooting rights over the land, or to any person who has the latter's authority in writing to make such a demand.

What the Act seems to be saying so far, is a tenant farmer can give a friend or a farm worker written permission to shoot hares and rabbits on his farm, but only one of them at any one time.

(4) No firearms must be used at night, from one hour after sunset to one hour before sunrise. This looks like night shooting for rabbits with a pickup or Land-Rover headlights is illegal.

(5) No spring traps must be set except in rabbit holes and no poison must be used.

Snaring and using ferrets to catch rabbits are all legal, but nothing is said in the Act about these methods of killing rabbits. You can see the reason why spring traps must be set inside rabbit holes as they could trap birds and cats.

(6) I find this section of the Act most interesting. On moorlands and unenclosed lands, not being arable lands, which either do not adjoin arable lands, or if they do are not less than twenty five acres in extent, then the rights can only be exercised from 11th December to the 31st March inclusive.

This is to protect the grouse as the grouse shooting season ends on the 10th December. So, if your farm joins a moor or open ground and is not arable and is twenty five acres or more, you can't shoot hares or rabbits between the 11th December and the 31st March as during this time the grouse will be sitting on eggs.

I cannot but think that the Act is very unsatisfactory, not so much about the laws it makes, but for what it leaves unsaid.

So many problems seem to present themselves to the inquiring mind that it is very difficult, if not impossible, to forecast the judicial answer to some cases when they come before the Courts for a decision.

What, for instance, is meant by a member of the occupier's *household*? Is a gardener who works for a tenant farmer and who sleeps in a cottage rented by the tenant, which is built on the land, a member of his *household*?

I think that such an implication of the word *household* is a good deal wider than the ordinary sense of the word. The meaning commonly attached to it, of persons dwelling under the same roof, is the one which is more likely to be adopted when the point comes before a High Court for a decision.

Again, what does *ordinary service* mean? Are a gang of labourers who are taken on for the harvest only, to be considered as in *ordinary service* of the farmer? If they are, the farmer can authorise each one of them to kill the ground game that have been making inroads upon his crops.

The authority above quoted seems to be of the opinion that *ordinary* would seem to mean 'regular'. If so a casual labourer who was employed for a few days at the harvest time would not come within this class, as he would not be in the ordinary employment. It must mean a person who was regularly employed on the farm.

I am inclined to think that farm labourers, who work for the farmer for the whole harvest, would be within the privileged class and would be allowed to shoot ground game on the farm.

Whilst a farm labourer, who is casually engaged by the day on the farm by the farmer at a busy time, would not be permitted to shoot ground game on the farm under the Act.

It must be remembered that members of the household must live on the land. Therefore if a man takes the tenancy of a farm without a farmhouse being attached to it, it will be practically impossible for him to authorise any of his household to exercise the powers of killing ground game unless they are in his ordinary service on the land.

If for instance, the tenant of a farm lives in another farmhouse on another farm, he may authorise his son who lives with him to kill ground game on the farm, if and only if, the son works on the land for his father.

The third heading of *One person bona fide employed for reward* (being paid), also presents great difficulties and what does it really mean? Must such a person only be fully employed on one farm before he can be authorised to shoot the ground game on that farm?

I think the legislators could hardly have meant to put such a narrow construction to the clause. For instance, a mole catcher who was employed to kill rats, moles and rabbits on the farm would be covered by the Act.

And, no doubt, so would a man who was not fully employed by a tenant farmer, but was paid so much a head for every rabbit he killed, and came onto the land for that purpose only at odd times when he had a mind to do so.

In the case above, one supposes a tenant farmer not living on the land, could give his son, who was not employed on the land, liberty to shoot or take ground game by employing him for reward (paying him).

It seems that he could do so if the employment was *bona fide*, but the case would certainly present a suspicious appearance and the circumstances would have to be strictly investigated, if the point was raised in Court.

If the magistrates were of the opinion that the tenant farmer was merely trying to evade the Act, in order to give his son a right of shooting, they would be bound to hold that the employment was not *bona fide*, and that the son was not a person privileged to exercise the powers of the Act.

The object of limiting the class of person to exercise the powers of the Act is of course to prevent the wholesale slaughter of the ground game, and to prevent injury to the landlord who has the sporting rights on the farm.

It must always be remembered that the Act was not passed to give farm tenants the sporting rights for pleasure, but merely to give them a substantial check on the power of the landlord, to keep the land from being overrun with pheasants and rabbits.

The Act applies to all occupiers of land who occupy the land as tenants and not as owners. The Act reads as follows. *In the interest of good husbandry and for the labour invested by the occupiers of the land to cultivate the soil, provision should be made to enable the occupier to protect their crops from injury and loss by ground game.*

The Act is pretty hard on some tenants. Take for instance the case of a market gardener who rents his land without any reservation of the game. He is possibly troubled by hares and rabbits which make short work of his young cabbages and lettuces.

He may set snares in the hedge for the hares as he could do before the Act, but he may not set spring traps for rabbits, or lay poison for them, nor may he go out on a moonlit night and take pot shots at them with firearms. All of his privileges have been taken from him without any rhyme or reason.

With regards to the moor-lands and unenclosed grassland. It will be remembered that the tenant's rights can only be exercised from 11th December to the 31st March inclusive. They may only shoot ground game between these dates.

This is evidently a concession to the grouse shooters, but its application is extended far beyond what is necessary to protect the grouse moors.

The terms of the sub-section of the Act are wide enough to cover the greater part of every mountain in the United Kingdom, as well as all the sand-hills on the coast and all the large village commons.

Chapter 6   POACHING

THE WILDCAT

Poaching is an occupation which had a great deal of charm about it in years gone by. Most country people with only a few acres of useless land either starved or went poaching just to survive.

There were many very poor families in the countryside, and poaching was the only way in which some families could taste a bit of meat or fish. However, if the poacher was caught the penalty was very severe.

It is recorded that during the 17th century a poacher caught shooting a deer in the Royal Forest of Athole, in Scotland, had one of his hands cut off. This was to stop him from using the longbow again, which was the poacher's weapon in those days.

Some poachers became well known and were hunted high and low, but they were most often a few steps ahead of the gamekeepers and the watchers. Poaching was a way of life for a few people and they poached for the pot.

As the punishment for poaching became more humane poaching became more widespread and the poachers devised all types of equipment to catch, shoot and trap meat and fish for the pot, as well as to sell.

The estates rearing game birds and ground game for sport were creating great opportunities for the poachers. Some of the estates built lethal man-traps on the estates to try and catch the villains.

There were many scrimmages between the gamekeepers and the poachers over the years. There are some very interesting stories recorded, about how some poachers went about catching and trapping game, and what they did with the game after they had caught and killed it.

The poachers of the past were very poor and if they had a family to keep, they had to get what they could just to survive. Some poachers were lazy and wouldn't work, so they would take and steal whatever they could get their hands on.

Although some poachers of the past caused many problems for the gamekeepers and for some estates, they were nothing like some of the poachers of today who are ruthless hardened criminals, who see the opportunity to make a quick buck by raiding estates and stealing hundreds of pheasants in one night, and then selling them.

FOLDING .410 SHOTGUN

These modern poachers don't steal for the pot to fill their bellies. They poach to fill their pockets. They are just a bunch of thugs who don't have a particle of sportsmanship in their veins.

The poachers use all sorts of guns, spikes, nets, motor-cars, sulphur, explosives and traps that will quickly reduce the game into their possession. They never think about the cruelty they can cause, that never enters the poachers' heads.

My father and I have had a taste of these poachers in the past. We have lost a lot of pheasants to them. Let me tell you a story about what some poachers once did to us.

My father used to hatch and rear about one hundred young pheasants every year. There were probably more than that number of wild birds on the shoot at any one time, as it was never over shot. We had about four shoots a year and probably a few nights at the ducks.

When the young pheasants were old enough my father and I used to put the young birds into a pen in the middle of the long plantation. The long wood was a mixture of hardwood and firs.

We used to feed the pheasants at various points throughout the wood. We also had some open rides cut across the wood and when we used to shoot the wood we would place some guns across the open rides and drive the pheasants from one end of the wood into the centre of the wood where the rearing pen was.

When we finished shooting one half of the wood we would then go to the other end of the wood and drive it into the middle. The guns standing on the open rides in the wood had some great sport, so did the guns that were walking along the outside of the wood.

The wood was two fields from the road, which was a B road and was little used. The shoot was fairly private. However this particular year we heard that there had been a lot of pheasant poaching from estates, and the stealing of sheep and equipment from farms.

Any surplus game my father had at the end of a day's shooting went to a local fishmonger who used to buy it from him. It was a good arrangement and every body was happy. It was the last week in October and we hadn't started shooting the pheasants by then.

Some of us looked at the pheasants every day and fed them if they needed some food. This particular Monday morning the phone rang, it was the fishmonger wanting to speak to my father.

The fishmonger told my father that he had just bought twenty pheasants from two strangers, who had said the pheasants had been shot on the Saturday on a nearby shoot.

The fishmonger said that after he had paid the strangers for the pheasants and he was sorting them out, he found that the pheasants hadn't been shot at all, and he found two of the cock pheasants had hen rings on their legs. He thought the birds must have come from my father's shoot.

My father's first reactions were that the pheasants couldn't be his birds as he hadn't started shooting yet. We dashed round to the wood to look at our pheasants.

Sure enough they were our pheasants all right, the fishmonger was correct. We found this long pole in the wood with a sharpened six inch nail hammered into one end. The poachers had used it to spear the pheasants in the back as they sat roosting on the lower branches of the trees on the Sunday night.

We lost about half our pheasants that year to poachers, they were never caught. The fishmonger only phoned up my father because he knew my father used to put a different coloured hen ring on a few cock pheasants every year, to keep in touch with what birds were left on the shoot.

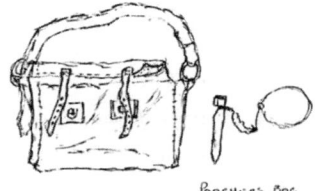
Poachers Bag & Snare

We lost a few more pheasants another night to poachers, which I will tell you about later in the chapter. The poachers had used a method to catch the pheasants that I had never come across before.

Most of the poaching for game is done at night, when the poachers know the woods are likely to be quiet and they hope and think the gamekeepers will be sitting in their cottages.

The gamekeepers are cunning and are always about, they try and keep one stride ahead of the poachers, which is very difficult. On some large estates where they rear thousands of pheasants every year, a regular army of night watchers are employed to try and prevent the night poachers from stealing the pheasants.

On a moonlit night pheasants sitting on a low perch fall easy victims, as a skilful hand can pick them off the trees one by one without disturbing the other birds, or making any noise, especially when the birds are not shot until late in the season.

The Night Poachers Act of 1828 very clearly lays down the definition of 'night'. It states that night shall be considered as at the first hour after sunset, and to conclude at the stroke of the last hour before sunrise.

Another Night Poaching Act was passed in 1844. This second Act was merely passed to extend the provisions of the 1828 Act to cover highways and roadsides and to remedy defects.

The 1844 Act states that all pains, punishments and forfeitures imposed by the Act of 1828 on persons taking or destroying game, or rabbits, by night in open or inclosed land, should be extended to the unlawfully taking, or destroying of game or rabbits on any public road, highway, or path.

These two Acts must be read and be construed together. In their interpretation by the Courts the following points have been laid down and explanations given.

'To take' means to catch or to kill, and not necessary to take away so as to deprive the lawful owner of the game so taken. It would appear that the section would apply to a tenant farmer, who unlawfully took or killed game which was reserved to his landlord, or to a lessee.

Rabbits are omitted from the second part of section 1 of the Act of 1828. (which deals with the offence of being on the land with intent).

It follows therefore that it is no offence to be on land at night with a gun, or nets, in search of rabbits, only if none are taken or killed. So if a poacher is caught at night with a gun or nets and if he hides the rabbits he has caught, and he denies he was in search of game, it could be very difficult to prosecute him.

Again, dogs are not mentioned in the Act, so that if no gun, net or other instruments (a snare for instance) is found, the presence of a dog will not tend towards a conviction even although it is seen chasing a hare.

Some wily poachers know the law pretty well. A poacher may go with a pal and wring the necks of any number of pheasants roosting in a wood, and his pal can safely get off with the birds whilst the poacher leads the gamekeepers a merry dance in the opposite direction.

If the gamekeepers happen to catch and arrest the poacher, and they can't bring forward any clear evidence of the actual taking of the birds, the poacher is pretty sure of an acquittal and will be free from punishment.

The gamekeepers know the pheasants have been taken, but they cannot prove it. Whilst the magistrates are satisfied that the poacher was in search of game, but cannot convict him owing to the absence of evidence and to the absence of any gun, or snares being found.

However if two poachers are out on a joint adventure and one of them stands on the road, whilst the other one goes onto the adjoining land with a gun and he is the only one proved to have taken game or rabbits, the other poacher can also be convicted.

Comparing the Night Poaching Act with the day poaching contained in the Game Act of 1831, I find the following difference. Assuming that no evidence of the actual taking of game or rabbits is forth coming, *in the daytime* the presence of a dog, or the carrying of a gun or net, or the setting of a snare, or a trap, either on another man's land or on the highway, may be sufficient to convict a man of an offence. The magistrates have to be satisfied that the defendant was in pursuit of game or rabbits.

At night, the fact of a dog being with the accused person is practically worthless evidence, likewise is the seizure of a net or spring traps, which are used almost entirely for rabbits, the pursuit of which is no offence. The magistrates would have to be satisfied that hares were not the intended quarry.

Again, at night, the pursuit of game is no offence without a gun, net, snare etc, and if on the highway or road, not even with these. A man may allow himself to be caught setting a snare for hares on a highway, but if he has not taken any at the time he himself is taken, then he is likely to go free.

Waste land does not appear to be within the Act of 1828. Apparently no offence can be committed at night on such land, though roadside wastes are, as a rule, part of the highway and so within the Act of 1844.

The last and most serious offence that is dealt with by the Night Poaching Acts, is that created by section 9 of the Act of 1828, which makes it a misdemeanour, punishable by penal servitude of up to fourteen years, or imprisonment with hard labour up to two years, for any three or more persons together, to unlawfully enter and be in any land whether open or inclosed for the purpose of taking or destroying game or rabbits. Any such persons being armed with a gun, cross bow, firearm, or any other offensive weapon.

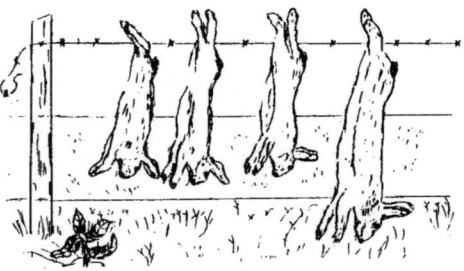

ARRESTING OF POACHERS

It is extremely important that all persons interested in the preservation of game should understand within what limits the right of arrest of offenders against the game laws may be exercised.

The common law gives no right to arrest a trespasser, though an owner or occupier of land may use sufficient force to evict a trespasser, if, on request he refuses to leave. The Game Act of 1831 and the Night Poaching Acts of 1828 and 1844 permit certain powers of arrest.

ARREST IN THE DAYTIME

No one may arrest a trespasser merely because he is trespassing, but certain persons are authorised to require any person found trespassing in pursuit of game to quit the land, and to give his given name and surname and place of abode.

In the event of the trespasser refusing to quit the land, or refusing to give his name and address, or giving a false name or address, or giving an address which is clearly insufficient to enable him to be found, he may be forthwith arrested and taken before a Magistrate.

The refusal of the trespasser to give the above particulars whether he be arrested on the spot, or not, entails a fine not exceeding £5 and costs, and in default of payment imprisonment with hard labour.

THE POACHING PREVENTION ACT 1862

On the 7th August 1862 a statute was passed for the prevention of poaching, which is a most useful enactment to game preservers and, although it may be brief in its provisions, the few sections it does contain are very much to the point.

As the Act is such a short one it will be clearer if I try and set out the gist of each section of the Act and make a few comments about it later.

Section 1. defines 'game' as any one or more hares, pheasants, partridges, eggs of pheasants and partridges, woodcock, snipe, rabbits, grouse, black or moor game, and the eggs of grouse, black or moor game.

Section 2. is most important for it empowers any constable or police officer in any county, borough, or place in Great Britain and Ireland, in any highway, street or public place, to search any person whom he may have good cause to suspect of coming from land where he shall have been unlawfully in search, or pursuit of game.

Or any person aiding or abetting such person, and of having in his possession any game unlawfully obtained, or any gun, part of a gun, or nets or engines used for the killing or taking of game.

The constable can also stop and search any cart, or other conveyance, in which the constable shall have good cause to suspect that any such game, or any such article, or thing is being carried by such a person.

Should the constable find any game or such article, or thing upon such person, cart or other conveyance, he may seize and detain such game, article, or thing.

The constable shall in such a case apply to some justice of the peace for a summons, citing such person to appear before two justices etc, in England and Ireland, and before a sheriff, or any two justices of the peace in Scotland.

If such person shall be found to have obtained such game by unlawfully going on any land in search or in pursuit of game, or to have used any such article or thing for unlawfully killing, or taking game, or being found to have been an accessory, on conviction the penalty will not exceed £5.

Fox

Along with the forfeiture of game, guns, part of guns, nets and engines, which the justices shall direct to be sold or destroyed etc, for the benefit of the treasurer of that particular county or borough. In the case of dismissal of the summons, the game or guns etc found on the person summoned are to be returned.

Sections 3,4,5, and 6 deal only with the recovery of the penalties and the methods of procedure.

I doubt whether this Act would ever have been passed had it not been for the numerous fights between gamekeepers and poachers which were so constantly reported in the press over a hundred years ago. This was around 1860 and at that time the shotgun saw new developments and the estates rearing game birds were becoming more organised.

Village loafers who had picked up the odd rabbit or two without much hindrance, found the vigilance of the gamekeepers and the watchers a nuisance and annoyance to them.

They were tempted by the preserves overstocked with game and banded themselves together into gangs and defied the law, which the jealousy of the non - sporting public had caused to be laid down in a very restricted manner.

The appearance of a police constable in Court in any game case was generally looked upon with great disapproval, but the Poaching Prevention Act of 1862 remedied this evil and appealed directly to the police for the protection of game. By its aid the country police became of great assistance to gamekeepers, where formerly they were more or less a hindrance.

A zealous police officer, ever eager to obtain a conviction to his credit, sometimes requires the odd tip or two as to where a poaching expedition is planned to be, so he can have the luck to fall in the way of it as it is returning homewards in the early hours.

The power to search any suspect person, and to stop and search any cart, is a mighty weapon in police hands and accounts for hundreds of cases which otherwise would never have been heard, because when game is found on the suspects the onus of accounting for its lawful possession falls upon their shoulders, and does not rest with the prosecution.

CATAPULT

TOOTH JAW TRAP

It will be seen that the definition of 'game' in the Act is a very wide one, including as it does rabbits, the eggs of game, woodcock and snipe, but the bulk of the cases that came before the Court were those where rabbits, pheasants, partridges, or in the summer, when the eggs of the latter were stolen.

If the 1862 Act is compared with the Night Poaching Act of 1828, it will be seen that a police constable may get a conviction where a gamekeeper could not.

Under the 1862 Act, it will be remembered, it is no offence to set snares for rabbits on land at night unless rabbits are actually caught. Therefore, if poachers are disturbed by the gamekeeper before they have caught anything, they cannot be convicted.

If, however, they are subsequently seen on the highway by a police constable, and they are searched and nets are found on them, a conviction must follow from the joint evidence of the keeper and the policeman.

Another advantage of the policeman's power is that there is no necessity to allege on what particular land the accused had been poaching. If, however, the poacher was seen on the highway by a gamekeeper, he must specify the particular land on which the game is alleged to have been taken.

It does not seem to have been decided as to what is included in the word 'land'. The accused must only be suspected to have come from some 'land'.

I believe the Act does not extend to actual poaching on the highway itself. Though there never has been a case in which a poacher has had the boldness to set up as a defence that he was not taking game on anyone's land, but on the highway.

A question that is often asked is: If you come across a dead pheasant, or partridge on the public road or highway, can you pick up the game and claim it as your property? I hope the following notes will answer that question.

Young game chicks unable to leave the nest, or at least the soil of their home, are the property of the owner of the soil. In all countries tame animals (or those which have been tamed) are the property of the person who keeps them.

Young pheasants hatched from the setting of eggs by a barn-door hen, are considered to be tame so long as they follow their mother. To steal them is therefore punishable as theft or larceny and they do not require the protection of the game laws.

Dead game also does not fall under the provisions of the game laws. It has therefore been decided in Scotland, that if a man was passing along a public road while pheasants were being shot on the adjoining land, and he picked up a dead pheasant which fell at his feet and walked off with it, he is not guilty of either theft or contravention of the game laws.

There is no decision quite so clear in England or Ireland, but the law is understood to be the same with regards to dead game. In England and in Ireland the property in game is sometimes affected by the peculiar privileges belonging to royal forests, chases, outlying parts, parks, free warrens and manors.

The keepers on such estates also have exceptional powers, but such privileged places are not so numerous as to require notice in Scotland.

Now back to my father and poaching. My father once told us over lunch that he once caught two old poachers in the pheasant wood (as we called it), burning sulphur at the bottom of two trees where pheasants had perched for the night.

The poachers also had a .410 single barrel shotgun with them, which my father managed to take from them. They didn't use the shotgun because of the noise it would make, so they thought they would try burning sulphur to bag a few roosting pheasants.

This is what these two thugs were up to when my father caught them red handed in the wood. It was a very quiet October evening, dusk was just

A COCKER SPANIEL

setting and the pheasants had just got perched for the evening.

There were about thirty pheasants perched on two or three trees, which were close together. The two poachers had a bag of sulphur each and they were just in the process of putting some sulphur on to two bits of tin under the trees where the pheasants were roosting. My father told us that the burning sulphur made the pheasants dizzy and the poachers could just pick them from the tree branches.

My father said the farm dogs had told him that something wasn't right that night and he set off alone to check the pheasant wood. He went straight to the part of the wood where he knew the pheasants would be roosting.

When he got to the wood one of the poachers had just lit the sulphur. He could smell this burning sulphur and when he saw the poachers he dashed straight at them, kicked the burning sulphur, which was letting off a pungent smell, and grabbed their .410 shotgun which was lying on the ground.

My father aimed the shotgun at the poachers and told them if they moved he would shoot them with their own shotgun, which was loaded. Both poachers stood still, afraid they might get shot, (something my father would never have done).

My father got both the names and addresses of the poachers. They had come from a village several miles away on bikes and had set out to bag a few pheasants for the pot and to sell them. Both poachers were miners and worked on shifts.

The poachers were reported to the police, but because they hadn't caught any pheasants at the time the police didn't convict them, but gave both of them a stern warning about their poaching expedition.

My father kept their shotgun and some of their sulphur, which was used quite a lot at one time mixed with nicotine and spread onto the backs of sheep to stop the spread of sheep scab.

Chapter 7   DEER

A RED STAG

Deer are lovely animals to watch and study. The coats of the deer blend in with their surroundings and they can sometimes be very difficult to spot. A deer farmer once told me that you can't drive deer like sheep or cattle because they just split apart.

I was at a deer farm in Scotland one day discussing with the farmer the problems he had with farming the Red deer. By coincidence, that morning as the farmer and I were standing in the farmyard at the time chatting, and he was just telling me how this stag had jumped out of the enclosure the previous day and had disappeared, we both just happened to be looking down the farm lane and there the stag was coming trotting back up the farm road.

The farmer said, 'Let me just go quickly and open the gate into the field where the hinds are.' The farmer was at the gate just before the stag and when he opened the closure gate the stag just trotted back into the pasture.

Some of the hinds looked up to see the stag trotting towards them, but they were unconcerned. It was the month of October when I visited the farm and this was the rutting season. The farmer explained that this was only a young stag who was trying to steal some hinds, but the master stag fought him off and the young stag had run and jumped out of the enclosure.

This farmer had a herd of two hundred and fifty Red deer, he reckoned about one stag to forty hinds. The deer are butchered on the farm when they are between a year and eighteen months old, and only the stags are killed and sold as venison. They kill out about 60 kg or 120 lbs.

The young yearling hinds are sold as breeding stock for about £400 each. A good breeding stag can cost around £2,500.

The hinds are fed lanzern nuts (a high protein cattle feed) in a trough during the summer, when they have a calf at foot, and potatoes during the winter along with a bit of good hay.

A Roe Buck

The rutting season starts in October and can last for nearly two months. The stags are a bit unpredictable during the rutting season and one has to be very careful and stay well clear of them.

The farmer selects a stag for venison, he then shoots it in the field with a rifle. It is all done very quietly. He then takes the deer into a small butchering house, which he built, where he skins and cuts it up into joints and puts them into the freezer. The venison cuts vary between £4 a pound and £5 a pound.

The farmer said he could sell all the venison he kills. People and shops order the venison over the phone and many people call at the farm for the venison. These Red deer could be classed as domestic animals, although they are still very wild animals.

I will tell you more about the Roe deer and the Red deer later in the chapter. These are the deer which I was mostly involved with. I have shot a number of Roe deer in the past with my father, he also used to stalk and shoot the Red deer. First of all, though, lets look at the laws and Acts relating to deer.

A Scottish Deer-Hound

Wild deer come under the common law rules as game, although they are not classed as game, and the occupier of any land, who sights a wild deer on his land, may shoot it and the deer will belong to him, (this could be a tenant farmer).

I am presuming of course that the sporting rights have not been reserved by the landlord or granted to any other person. For in such case the right to take the deer would belong to them.

It must be remembered however that deer are not included in the definition of 'game', so that a mere reservation of game would not include deer. (Which means wild deer are not classed as game).

Tame deer on the other hand are as much a species of private property as sheep and cattle, so if a tame deer strays onto another man's land he has no right to shoot or take it against the real owner.

If he does he may be prosecuted for stealing, if it was shown that he knew it to be a tame animal, but it would be difficult to secure a conviction if the plea were set up that the shooter imagined it was a wild deer.

In such a case, it would have to be considered whether there were any wild deer within such a distance, as to make it reasonable to suppose that the one shot by the landowner, or the tenant farmer, was a wild animal.

ROEBUCK

It is well known that a deer, wild or tame, will on occasion travel a very long distance from the woods or parks in which it is usually to be found.

Although ignorance of the fact that the animal was a tame one may remove the act of killing, or taking it, from the category of a criminal offence, the right to the carcass of the deer when killed will not depend upon the knowledge or the belief of the shooter, but upon the fact as to whether the deer was in reality a tame one or not.

If it was a tame one, the carcass of the deer will belong to the owner of the live deer; if it was a wild one it will belong to the shooter or to the person on whose land it was shot.

Some difficult question may arise at this point. A pet deer is undoubtedly a tame one, and so are the stags that are kept for hunting purposes. On the other hand stags which have travelled from such regions as the New Forest, or from Exmoor, certainly fall within the category of wild deer.

The difficulty arises when it comes to consider the position of deer in parks. In many cases, especially in small parks, the deer are practically tame, or as tame as they can be made when kept in herds, and to knowingly steal or kill and take a deer belonging to one of such herds, appears to be as much stealing the deer at common law, as is the stealing of a pet deer.

No doubt all park owners would contend, (if there were an advantage in doing so), that their herds were sufficiently tamed to be classed as domestic animals and be protected by the law.

However, in very large parks, woods and forests it is undoubtedly the fact that we often find the deer absolutely wild. In such cases it could hardly be held that they are ranked as domestic animals. In each case, however, it is a question of fact to be determined by the judge or magistrate.

Wild deer, like game proper, were not the subject of property at common law, (which means deer are not game) and it was no offence to kill deer on another man's land. The only remedy the owner had of such land was to bring a common law action for trespass.

Various provisions have from time to time been made by Act of Parliament to protect the interests of deer preserves. The older statutes were repealed and replaced by the Larceny Act of 1861 (Sections 12 to 16).

The first of the above sections of this statute relates to deer in a legal forest, hunting grounds, or out-lying parts (the borders of a legal forest).

A penalty of any sum, not exceeding £50, is enforceable on anyone found unlawfully and wilfully killing, hunting, snaring or wounding, or attempting to kill or wound any deer being kept on the above grounds.

The next section throws the protection of the criminal law round the deer kept in a park etc, provided that they stay there.

Anyone found unlawfully and wilfully coursing, hunting, snaring, carrying away, killing or wounding, or attempting to kill or wound any deer kept, or being in the enclosed part of any forest etc, or in any enclosed land where deer shall usually be kept, is guilty of a felony and liable to imprisonment up to two years with or without hard labour. If the male is under 16, with, or without, whipping.

Section 13. This section protects wild deer, as tame deer are already protected by the common law.

Section 14. This section is a very useful section. It provides, in effect, that any person in whose possession, or on whose premises any deer, or the head, skin, or other part of any deer, or any snare or engines for taking deer is found, may be summoned before a justice of the peace to account for the same.

If he fails to give a good account showing that he came by the same lawfully, and in the case of a snare or engine for taking deer, that he did not keep the same for an unlawful purpose, or he may be fined up to £20.

If the person so summoned proves that he innocently obtained the deer, or its head, or its skin etc from another person, then the last mentioned person may be summoned to prove his innocence.

This game could go on and on, and when the magistrates finally gets someone before him who cannot account for the possession, in a legal manner, of the deer, he may be fined.

Section 15. provides a penalty not exceeding £20, *for unlawfully and wilfully setting or using any snare, or engine for the purpose of taking deer in any forest, hunting grounds or out lying parts (the borders of a legal forest), or in any inclosed land where deer are usually kept, or for unlawfully and wilfully destroying any part of any fence on land where deer are usually kept.*

I find it very interesting that where anyone is found to be wilfully destroying any part of any fence on land where deer are usually kept, they will be fined a penalty not exceeding £20. A poacher or anyone could just be destroying a fence where deer are kept just for spite.

Section 16. provides that *if any person shall enter any forest etc, or inclosed land where deer are usually kept with the intent to unlawfully hunt, course, wound, kill, snare, or carry away any deer, then every person entrusted with the care of such deer and any of his assistants, may demand from the offender any gun, firearms, snares, or engines, or any dog brought for hunting, coursing, or killing deer.*

If the same is not immediately delivered up, the person may seize and take the same from him, or if the offender escapes, he may be followed and taken at any other place.

Moreover to protect the forester or park-keeper and his assistant, it is provided that if the offender shall beat any of them whilst in the execution of the powers given by the Act, he shall be guilty of a felony (a serious offence), and be liable to imprisonment with or without hard labour, for not exceeding two years.

The provisions of this Act are intended for the protection of wild deer. Tame deer, as mentioned above, are under the protection of the common law. It will be seen that the Act only refers, in the case of inclosed lands, to those inclosures where deer are usually kept.

If, however, a wild deer is found upon an ordinary farm and is shot by a trespasser, the occupier has no criminal remedy against the trespasser, but he may, of course, bring a useless and expensive common law action for trespass.

On the other hand, the trespasser has no right to the carcass of the deer, which belongs to the occupier of the land, (unless the general sporting rights belong to the landlord or to some other person).

The following is a story about a farmer who went to see *The Poacher's Lawyer* about a deer that was shot on his land. I hope you enjoy the story and what the law had to say about the deer.

A farmer had seen a fine fat doe grazing in one of his pastures. Being anxious for a bit of sport and a bit of venison, he took his gun and quickly loaded it with some special heavy cartridges and made for a corner of the field where the deer was grazing some distance away.

The farmer started creeping cautiously along under the shadow of the hedge, when he heard a shot being fired and when he looked up he saw the deer bound into the air and fall dead.

A moment after, a well-known poacher proceeded leisurely to crawl through another hedge at a spot much nearer to the dead deer.

This was too much for the farmer, who rushed forward and who would have committed a violent assault on the trespasser, on the spot, had not the poacher decided it was best to leave without delay.

The farmer at once cut the deer's throat and then sent it

to the village butcher to be skinned and cut up. That same day the farmer went to see *The Poacher's Lawyer* to get some advice about what he could do about the poacher.

The farmer asked the lawyer, 'Could he prosecute the poacher for stealing?' 'No,' said the lawyer. 'Then,' said the farmer, 'could he prosecute him for trespass in pursuit of game?'

The lawyer said, 'My dear sir, deer are not game.' The farmer said, 'Not game? Then what do we mean, when we talk about big game, surely that includes deer?'

The lawyer said, 'When I say 'game' of course I mean game as defined by the Game Acts, and there appears to be no provision in the Acts to meet such a case as this.'

Shortly before the farmer visited his office the lawyer had heard a rumour of the circumstances and had had an opportunity of looking the point up, otherwise he would not, perhaps, have been so ready with the answer.

The farmer continued, 'Surely a wild deer belongs to me when it comes on my land? At least so I read somewhere.'

The lawyer said, 'No doubt it does, my dear sir, when it is killed, but not until.' (Remember wild birds and animals belong to no one when they are alive and free). 'Are you quite sure it was a wild deer?'

'Well,' said the farmer, 'I've really never thought about it till now and as you come to raise the question, perhaps it wasn't a very wild deer. Supposing it wasn't wild, what then?'

'Well then,' said the lawyer, 'the owner might come and claim the deer carcass.'

So the farmer asked, 'And suppose that the deer was already eaten?'

'Well,' replied the lawyer, 'It might be that the owner of the dead deer would come on you for the value of it.'

The farmer considered what the lawyer had told him and thought he would enquire about the deer.

The farmer then informed the local police about the deer. The policeman advised that he would make some enquiries as to who the owner of the deer was and said, 'The owner of the deer, if we find him, might prosecute that scoundrel of a poacher for shooting a tame deer.'

The policeman's enquiries were soon well rewarded and the venison was well hung up before Lord Brook's gamekeeper appeared on the scene and identified the skin at the butcher's as that of a doe that had escaped from his Lordship's park, some forty miles away, by leaping the park wall.

The farmer urged the keeper on to prosecute the shooter of the deer, but very wisely he refused, saying that, although he called the deer tame, he didn't know what the lawyers would make it out to be, and he knew that the poacher couldn't be convicted for shooting a wild deer outside the park.

Moreover, continued the keeper, once a deer had escaped as this one had, the park fence would never keep it in again. It would always be leaping the wall and he was glad it was shot.

All the keeper wanted was the skin of the deer and he suggested an equal division of the carcass between the farmer, the poacher, the butcher and the policeman.

The deer was shared out amongst the four to the satisfaction of all parties, except for the farmer who strongly objected to the poacher getting a share.

But as the farmer was not prepared to support his original contention that the animal really was a wild one, he had to give way and be content with the quarter allotted to him as his share of the spoil, (this would be unlikely to happen today).

The law about the shooting of wild deer and tame deer, or park deer is quite clear. Once it has been established that it is a wild deer or a tame deer that has been shot, then the appropriate action can be taken.

young deer fawns

Now let me tell you something about the Roe deer and the Red deer, which I have been involved with many times. I have shot a number of Roe deer on my father's shoot, because there were too many and they had started to damage young trees and shrubs.

First the Roe deer. This small deer is quite common throughout the country, although it is scarce in some parts of the country and more common in others.

The male Roe deer is called a buck, never a stag, and he grows antlers. The female is called a doe, never a hind. Young Roe deer of either sex are called kids or fawns, not calves.

An adult Roebuck will stand just over 2 feet at the shoulder and weigh about 50 lbs. The does are smaller and weigh about 40 lbs when they are fully grown.

The summer coat of the Roe deer is a brownish Red, short and very tight. In the winter their coat varies through many shades of grey.

When the fawns are born they have white spots on their backs, the spots vanish with the change of coat in the first autumn when they are about three months old or thereabouts. A fawn born in May should be clear of the spots in August.

In their winter coat many Roe deer have a white patch on the throat and another on the gullet. These marks are very common in the Scottish Roe deer of all ages when they're in their winter plumage.

The antlers of the Roebuck don't grow much longer than about 9 inches. Their antlers usually have three points each.

The antlers are made of bone and are cast and regrown each year. Adult Roebucks usually cast their antlers during the month of November.

The new antlers begin to grow almost at once, and during the growing period the antlers are covered with a furry coat, which is called velvet. A Roebuck at this time is said to be 'in velvet'.

When the antlers are fully grown, the velvet begins to

strip. The buck helps the stripping by rubbing its antlers against shrubs and trees. The new antlers are clear of velvet, or 'clean' as we say it, from almost the end of March onward.

The young bucks usually cast their antlers later than the old ones and they 'clean' later. Some young bucks may be in velvet well into May.

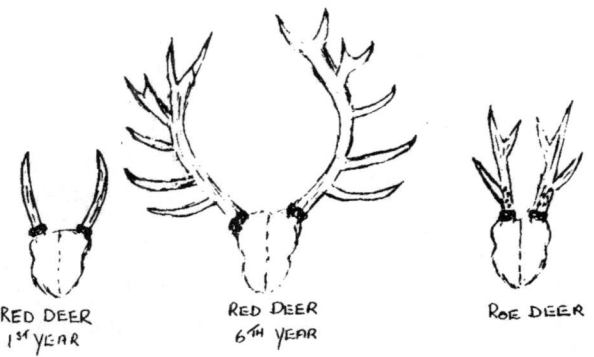

RED DEER 1st YEAR   RED DEER 6TH YEAR   ROE DEER

Fawns at a year old may have no more than simple spikes a few inches or so long, or they may have simple forks.

The Roebuck and doe are paired in June. That is to say the bucks begin to take an interest in the does in their territory. The rut, which is the real breeding season, is in July and August.

Near the end of August the bucks sometimes leave the does for a time, rejoining them in October or November. From then, until the spring, the family group may stay more or less together. You may even find Roe deer in small herds of half a dozen or more.

In their daily lives Roe deer are creatures of fairly regular habit. They may spend the whole of their lives within a two mile radius of where they were born, or to a certain place that they like.

They like young plantations, birch thickets, scrub land, or forests with plenty of cover. They also like to be near open areas where they can eat fresh green grass.

Because Roe deer like small plantations and shrubs, they can do a lot of damage if they are not controlled and they have to be culled. It's very sad to shoot such lovely animals, but it's necessary to keep their numbers under control, because of the amount of damage they can do to young trees and shrubs.

My father used to arrange a Roe deer shoot at various times when the Roe deer numbers had increased, on the shoot, and the deer were becoming a bit of a problem.

I can remember when I was about fifteen years old, my father arranged a Roe deer shoot. I was given one of his guns and was to join in with the other four shooters. My father had arranged a few drives and the deer were going to be driven to the guns.

I was placed behind an old oak tree and was told only to shoot the deer either in the heart, or in the head, but preferably in the head. I hadn't long to wait when I saw two deer heading straight for me.

I waited and waited until the deer were right close in on me, then I lifted my gun and aimed at the first deer and shot it in the head, it dropped stone dead. The second deer coming behind turned when the shot was fired, but I aimed and also shot it stone dead through the head.

When this drive was over. I looked down on these dead creatures that I had just shot, and turned to my father and asked if we really needed to shoot these lovely animals. My father replied that we had to, because there are too many of them and they were causing too much damage to the trees.

As I grew older, I soon discovered the amount of tree damage the Roe deer could do, and I was in favour of culling some of the deer, but only when it was necessary.

The Red deer is a much bigger deer than the Roe deer and is not found in as many parts of the country. The main herds of the Red deer are in the Highlands and Islands of Scotland, although there are pockets of wild Red deer in other parts of the country.

The Red deer male is called a stag and stands over four feet at the shoulder and the stags can weigh anything from twelve to twenty five stones, some mature stags can even weigh heavier than that.

Red deer stags are usually named according to the number of tines or points on their antlers. A stag with four points on each beam is an eight pointer. A stag with twelve points is a 'Royal' and a stag with fourteen points is called an 'Imperial'.

The female Red deer is called a hind and a newly born young deer is called a calf. From the calf stage to maturity a male Red deer has many names, which vary according to the area they live in.

For instance, a young stag with his first spikes is called a 'knobber' in the Highlands, and a 'pricket' in England, but there are no hard and fast rules.

Unlike the Roe deer, the Red stag casts his old antlers in the spring. He is just beginning to grow his new antlers when the Roebuck has his full antlers cleaned and hard. The Red deer stag roars like a lion, while the smaller Roebuck barks like a dog.

When you are stalking the Red deer out on the hills, you should always bear in mind the following. Red deer have a wonderful vision and can see you a long way off. Their hearing is also excellent and their sense of smell is very acute. You can never take any liberties with the Red deer's sense of smell.

I have been stalking Red deer with my father on many occasions, and have crawled on my belly and hands and knees for many a hundred yard.

The keepers who took us stalking Red deer varied a great deal. Some keepers were very chatty while others never said very much at all. The older keepers seemed to be the most interesting to be with, as they would tell us all about the weather, the hills and about the movements of the deer.

THE SPARROW HAWK ON
ITS PLUCKING POST

I was just a young boy at the time and, as usual, I was doing all the humping and carrying, but I learnt a great deal about the Red deer and the hills from the keepers and my father.

I can well remember some notes about deer stalking hanging in our back kitchen in a frame, which my father had done with a few simple drawings. This is what he said, which is still true today

(1)   Never attempt to stalk Red deer down wind.

(2)   Remember Red deer move up into the wind when they are feeding.

(3) Always try and stalk deer down the hill as they seldom look up the hill.

(4) When stalking deer try and keep the sun on your back.

(5) Do not stalk on a windy day as the deer dash about all over the place.

(6) When making a stalk check behind for deer higher up.

(7) In fine weather the biggest stags are on the high hills and in wet stormy weather they can be found on the lower ground.

(8) Remember whatever way the wind is blowing across the hills, there is always a current moving up and down the narrow glens.

(9) The distance one may approach near to a deer herd varies. When there is a strong wind blowing it may not be safe to pass within a mile of the herd.

(10) Always wear good warm clothes which blend in with the surroundings and which make little noise.

Chapter 8   ROOKS

THE Rook

Rooks are one of Britain's commonest large black birds. They nest in nearly every county of the British Isles except in the Shetlands. In 1903 there was a large rookery at the Marble Arch in London, which has long gone.

The last rookery in London, at Lee Green, was deserted in 1947. During the 1940's it was estimated that there were about three million rooks nesting in England, Scotland and Wales.

This information came from a survey covering every square mile of two-thirds of the British Isles taken between 1944 and 1946. They found every rookery in the area, and they counted the number of occupied nests.

It was really a very big job and nearly four hundred people took part in the survey and they were nearly all volunteers. They had to be very careful not to start before all the rook nests were built, and not to go on after the leaves had come out on the trees.

It was quite certain that this was the largest population of rooks to nest in Britain and there were less rooks nesting ten years earlier. This increase of rooks, of about 25%, was probably connected with the war time revolution in agriculture when the land had to be ploughed out to produce food.

I've had many a good night shooting young rooks when they were sitting out on the branches just before they could fly. It was well known among the farming community that on the 13th May the young rooks would be sitting out on the branches beside their nests, just before they took to the wing.

The 13th May was also the term day, known as the 'May Term', when the farm workers changed farms. This is when some farm workers, and some sportsmen got the job of shooting the young rooks.

Two or three days shooting away at the rooks soon reduced their numbers, but whether this had much effect on the overall rook numbers, I very much doubt. Some people that have a rookery on their land won't hear tell of having the young rooks shot as they like to see them.

I have shot young rooks at a number of rookeries by permission of the owners who were mainly farmers. The rooks used to do a lot of damage to their farm crops of oat, barley and wheat.

Rooks

I can well remember, not so many years ago, I started shooting the young rooks at this fairly large rookery for the farmer, because of the noise they were making and because of the damage the adult rooks were doing to his cereal crops.

I had been watching the rookery from early March, while

the parent birds were repairing and building new nests. There were one hundred and two nests in this rookery and the noise the birds were making would have wakened the dead.

Once the female rooks had laid their four or five eggs and were sitting on them, a bit of peace and calm was restored to the neighbourhood.

The hen birds alone sit on the eggs for about two and a half weeks, during which time they are fed by the cock birds. Most rook eggs hatch out by the middle of April.

When the young rooks hatch out the cock bird feeds them and the hen bird, but after a week and a half when the young are less naked and beginning to get some feathers, both parents come with their throat-pouches stuffed with food, mainly cereals and beetles.

By the 13th May, a little over four weeks after they hatch the young rooks become 'branchers', as they hop about the rookery from branch to branch just before they can fully fly.

Its about this time of year, the 13th May, that you can start shooting the young rooks and some of the adult birds, if you can get them. The parent birds will circle high above the nests if they catch sight of you in the rookery.

To try and shoot adult rooks flying above the rookery with a rifle is nearly impossible. I normally use a .22 rifle for shooting rooks. The young rooks sitting out on the branches, unable to fly, can be difficult enough to shoot with a rifle.

Some farmers use shotguns, they blast away at the nests, and if any young or adult birds are sitting in the nests they are killed. A shotgun makes a lot of noise, and the parent birds may leave the rookery altogether for a bit while the shooting goes on.

At this rookery I was using a rifle which only made a sharp crack. The parent birds just circled above the rookery. The leaves were fully on the trees by then and sometimes a parent bird would drop back down onto the nest, and I got a shot at it, but didn't always hit them.

I was shooting away at these young rooks on this quiet summer evening and I was standing underneath a tree in the rookery where a number of nests were above me. I had just shot this young rook and as it started to fall to the ground, I couldn't really see where it was falling for the leaves on the tree. Suddenly this dead bird hit me on the face and broke my glasses in two. This cost me over a £100 for a new pair of glasses, (a very expensive rook).

I had a few good nights' sport at this rookery before the young birds took to the wing. For many years this became a regular event. A few farmer friends and I used to have some good fun shooting rooks, and at the same time we were trying to reduce and control these pests for the farmers.

Rooks are very clever birds. I have many times watched them attack fields of standing wheat, barley, or oats, which were just turning from the green to the yellow stage, when the grain still has a soft milky texture.

A group of about thirty or forty rooks, would sit in a row along the fence top, or along the hedge top beside a field of wheat, barley, or oats. Then one of the rooks would drop down and pull one of the heads of grain over onto the ground, a wonderful skill

This was very cleverly done. Then another rook would follow and drop down and pull another head of grain over onto the ground. Before long the whole group were pulling heads of grain over, until they had a strip down several metres long, along the fence or hedge side.

I have spent a lot of time in the past, during the summer, shooting rooks and woodpigeons from fields of wheat, barley and oat crops, to keep the birds from eating and damaging the crops.

Woodpigeons are not as clever as rooks, they only attack the flattened parts of the crop after the rooks, or a strong wind and heavy rain flattens part of the crop.

It can be very difficult to get into a position to watch rooks pulling down the heads of a cereal crop. You have to be watching for the cereal crop to change colour and watching for the rooks sitting in line along a fence or hedge next to a standing crop.

The signs are always there as the rooks will very often sit along the fence beside a standing cereal crop for days on end. Then one day, usually first thing in the morning, the rooks will start to attack the crop.

When the rooks start to attack a cereal crop, it all happens very quickly and within an hour or two a group of rooks can have a large strip of the crop pulled down.

To see this actually happening with the rooks you have to be in a hide, either up a tree or along the hedge bottom. You have to do a bit of reconnaissance well before hand and get prepared, without the rooks seeing you.

I have watched a group of rooks pulling down half ripe cereals many times, they are very destructive birds. Once they get a taste of the soft milky cereals, they will keep visiting the field every day stripping the heads off the crop.

You can shoot and scare the rooks from a cereal crop that they have started to attack. Once you fire a shot at them they seem to scarper and don't return until you have gone.

Rooks won't decoy the same as woodpigeons. I have tried this many times, setting out a dead rook or two among the pigeon decoys. Some rooks will certainly come and have a look, but they are clever enough to keep well out of gun range.

THE SLOE.

Rook pie is a dish many country people will have heard of, but never tasted. My mother used to make the odd rook pie, and looking back it was a bit like hot pot with two or three young rooks in the pie.

Hot pot is a mixture of vegetables and meat. Well my

mother's rook pie was a bit like that, and it was very tasty indeed. Although I never heard the family rave on about her rook pies, we just ate what was served up. We normally had rook pie in the summer when the young rooks were about.

Although it is much darker, rook meat tastes a bit like chicken. When you come to think about it, rooks have a similar diet to chickens. The rooks' main diet is cereals - barley, wheat and oats, and the lesser part of their diet, which is about 25 %, is made up of beetles and insects.

It is in many cases easier to count rook nests than to count the number of rookeries, because it sometimes can be difficult to decide where one rookery starts and ends.

A rookery is where the rooks nest in the spring and a roost is a wood where the rooks sleep at night.

In England, in some areas, rooks nest in mile long strips down lines of trees, although most rookeries are not very large not many having more than one hundred nests and very few have more than four or five hundred nests.

In Scotland there are some rookeries with over a thousand nests in them and some many more. In 1945, in the Crow Wood, near Turriff in Aberdeenshire, there were 6,085 nests in the rookery. There are also some very large rookeries to be found in Germany, maybe not as big as the Crow Wood.

In the autumn the rook families all join up into much larger groups, than the rookery groups, and these groups form roost units in woods. There were once about 500 rook roosts in Britain, but the roost numbers have been reduced because of the changes in agriculture. Some roosting woods have been pulled down and the land ploughed up to grow more cereals.

In some areas it is possible to find out what rookeries belong to which roost. In the autumn evenings in particular, especially in October, some of the rooks which were that year's hatched birds visit their rookery and mess about with the old nests before making their way back to the roost woods.

Rooks stick to the same flight line and, as the light fades at dusk, you can watch these birds making for their roosts. I often see rooks passing over my head when I am out duck shooting waiting for the evening flight.

The rooks stream pass me, many times just over my head. Sometimes I see large groups passing overhead, and other times there are a string of birds flying overhead which lasts until its nearly dark.

I have tracked groups of rooks at dusk making for their roost. Some of the roosts are ancient sites and are many times not the rookeries. The roost sometimes is a large wood with mixed hardwood trees and there can be thousands of rooks, jackdaws and woodpigeons roosting in the same wood.

The rooks spend a lot of time feeding in grass fields. Then in the spring of the year they feed on the cereal seeds that have just been sown. In the summer they feed a lot on the partly ripe wheat, barley and oat crops.

With the changes in agriculture a lot of the winter cereal crops are now sown in August, September and October. The rooks would be feeding on the stubble fields at this time of year; but as many stubble fields are now ploughed over and re-sown with cereal seeds, including rape seeds, the rooks have plenty of food available to see them more or less right through the winter.

The Poppy

In 1944 and 1945 a sample survey of 1,577 rooks in England were looked at to see what they were eating. After making an allowance that insect matter is digested almost four times as fast as plant matter, it was found that the rooks eat 18% of insect matter and 82% of plant matter, which was mainly corn, wheat and barley. In the 1940's, however, it was mainly corn that was grown and from the survey it was thought that the rooks got most of the oats from the stubble fields.

Today there is very little corn grown, it is mainly barley, wheat and oilseed rape. There are a lot more cereals grown and the rooks probably do more damage today, to standing cereal crops, than they did in the 1940's.

The Rook

There are some weird tales about the lives of rooks which seem very strange. Ever heard of a 'Rooks Parliament'? This is thought to come about when a freak, or wounded bird, sitting on its own is mobbed and surrounded by a circle of other birds.

I have seen rooks sitting in circles on a grass field and I have also seen them sitting in a long row along a wire fence, or along a hedgerow, and also diving down and cawing at a dead bird lying on the ground.

The rooks make a cawing noise both at the rookery and at the roosting wood. At the rookery when the young birds are 'branchers' the adult birds make a lot of other noises from alarm calls, to yelps, hoots and song like calls.

The rook is a large, black bird with a bare face. It also has a baggy trouser appearance from the thigh feathers and is heavy looking in flight, it also steps sideways on the ground.

Compared with the raven, which is the largest black bird, a rook can be distinguished from other crows by its huge size. It is about the size of a buzzard. It flies rather heavily, but it often soars and performs remarkable aerobatics in the sky.

The ravens have a legend of their own. For many centuries ravens have guarded the Tower of London. History has it that should the ravens ever leave, The White Tower would crumble and a great disaster would befall England.

Fortunately, since the reign of King Charles II, these respected ravens have been protected by royal decree.

The Tower ravens reached their lowest point soon after World War II, because of the bombing in London and the unresolved kidnapping of 'Mabel'. The only raven left holding the fort was called 'Grip'.

New raven recruits were soon on their way to The Tower until it had its full complement of birds again. In recent years the ravens at The Tower have produced new generations of young birds.

The Raven

Some people with a rookery don't shoot the young rooks, nor will they allow anybody else to shoot them either. No matter about the noise the rooks make and the damage they do in the neighbourhood to crops.

So lets look at the past and present laws on rooks. To what extent has a man a property in rooks which congregate on his land?

How far is a man's rookery entitled to the protection of the law?

Has he any right of action against another man who maliciously disturbs the rooks, and what, if anything, is his remedy against killing rooks on his land?

Here is a case which will help to explain the position. A tenant farmer (lets call him Mr Miller) went to see *The Poacher's*

Lawyer one fine spring morning to get some advice about rooks and his rights.

Mr Miller the tenant farmer was no fool. When he visited the lawyer, he had thought about what questions he wanted to ask him, and he took his farm lease along, just in case it was needed.

Mr Miller, opened his questions by telling the lawyer that there were some friction between him and his landlord over the game on the farm, which was reserved to the landlord.

What Mr Miller wanted to know was what were his rights with regards to certain things on his farm that were not game, as he wanted to exercise his rights to their fullest extent in retaliation for his unjust treatment by the landlord.

After dealing with one or two other subjects Mr Miller said, 'Now, I want to know whether I can kill his rooks. The landlord has a rookery in a wood in his own occupation that joins the bottom end of my farm. The rooks come onto my farm and eat the crops. I have not shot any of the rooks yet as I keep a boy to frighten them off the corn.'

The lawyer said, 'Now Mr Miller, the landlord has no right to the rooks when they get on your farm, and of course your lease doesn't reserve them to him, so you can shoot them when they are on your corn to your heart's content.'

'Yes', replied Mr Miller, (as his face assumed an innocent looking smile) 'I hadn't much doubt about that. You must remember that one of my fields, a grass field, is next to the rookery. Now, if anyone stood in that grass field under the hedge alongside the wood, he might perhaps kill more rooks than was necessary to protect his corn.'

The lawyer replied, 'I get your drift Mr Miller. What you really want to know, is whether anyone, I won't say

115

you, but anyone else standing in your grass field can shoot the landlord's rooks as they come out of the wood and would this be legal?'

'No,' continued the lawyer, 'it is not legal, you would be liable to an action. Because you can't shoot over another man's land. If there is a right to shoot the rooks over your farm, there is no right to shoot over your landlord's land. That itself is a common law trespass. At least it is so considered by the best authorities, and if frequently repeated, the landlord might get an injunction against you for damages. If the rooks are killed at all, the shooting must be over your land.'

'Ah,' said Mr Miller, 'that is worth knowing. I shall take care to remember it in future.'

The lawyer said, 'The law makes a distinction between animals fit for food and those which are not, and between those which have received protection by common law, or by statute and those which have not.'

It is not alleged in this declaration that these rooks were fit for food, and we know for a fact that they are not generally so used.

Rooks are not protected by any statute, on the contrary, they have been declared by legislation to be a nuisance in the neighbourhood to where they are.

That being so, it is quite clear that no person can claim to have rooks resort to his lands, nor can any person become a wrongdoer by preventing them from doing so.

The following case, was about ducks, but bears a strong resemblance to rook shooting, lets you see what the law said.

The case was brought because a person was discharging guns near a decoy duck pond. This was to frighten the ducks from landing on the pond and was stopping the owner of the pond from getting a shot at them.

In the first place, it is observable that wildfowl are protected by the statute, and that they constitute a known article of food, and that a person keeping up a decoy pond spends money and time and the duck can be eaten by the general public.

It is a profitable way of employing land and was considered by Lord Holt as a description of trade. The case therefore stands on a different foundation from that of rooks.

Therefore the landlord had no property in these rooks in his rookery, as they are destructive in their habits and are not protected either by common law or statute, and the landlord is at no expense in regards to them.

The Poacher's Lawyer is of the opinion that the landlord had no right to insist upon having the rooks in his neighbourhood, and that he cannot maintain an action against a tenant farmer who shot them because they were eating his crop.

Chapter 9   TRESPASSING

We have all at one time in our lives trespassed onto another man's land. Most people that have trespassed would likely be unaware that they had done so.

Every day many people will be trespassing on another man's land when they think they have a right to be where they are.

There are thousands of people every day out walking in the countryside and a lot of these walkers will trespass onto another man's land. They may only put one foot off the public footpath, but they are still trespassing.

Then there are the people who go trespassing in pursuit of game, or they go trespassing to steal something. The poachers trespass all the time when hunting, shooting and trapping game.

There is a lot of thieving and stealing going on in the countryside these days, sheep, cattle, farm equipment, tools and game birds are all targeted. The thugs and thieves who steal from the countryside have to trespass to get the spoils and it's mainly all for gain.

This thieving from the countryside is a very big problem today and although the farmers and landowners are taking action to try and stop the thugs from thieving, at the present time the thieves seem to be winning.

Most people that trespass don't do any harm, but at the same time they have no right to be walking over another man's land without his permission. Trespassing over another man's land is not a big problem, but trespassing in pursuit of game, and to steal, is a very big problem.

The old smithy by the drove road at Muggleswick.

TRESPASS AT COMMON LAW

There are so many fallacies about what a trespass is that I will start with Trespass At Common Law, and what it is.

It is thought, by many, that so long as a man does no appreciable damage, he may roam about another man's land at his own sweet will.

This of course is not so, and the least entry into another man's property is a trespass. Throwing a stone into his field is as much a trespass as throwing it through a window of his house.

Likewise it is a common law trespass to shoot on to another man's land, or to send a dog on to it. In all such cases the law presumes a nominal damage if no appreciable injury has been done, and for such damage an action lies against the trespasser.

Actions at law are very expensive and hence are never brought against the ordinary so-called trespasser. A trespass likely to be brought before magistrates only arises where actual damage has been done to land, or to something growing, or affixed to it, such as grass, or crops, or fences.

Very slight damage will suffice - a few branches broken in the hedge, the grass appreciably injured or the like, but damage there must be. What the law is saying is, it is a waste of money taking a man to court for only trespassing on your land.

A prosecution before the magistrates is not for trespass in itself, but for malicious damage to real, or personal property, under the Malicious Injuries to Property Act of 1861.

If, therefore a man merely walks across your park, garden, wood, or across your stubble field, you cannot prosecute him before a magistrate. Your only legal remedy is an action at law, which has been hinted at as being useless in ninety-nine cases of trespass out of a hundred, on the grounds of the expense.

Further than this the Malicious Injuries to Property Act does not extend to products of the soil, which are entirely uncultivated, but come up spontaneously.

Consequently, you cannot prosecute before the magistrates the children you find picking violets or bluebells which grow wild in your woods, nor the man who scours your fields for mushrooms, unless, in either case, you can prove a hedge, trees, or fence etc was broken.

Just to digress for a moment. The milk quota, which was

brought into force in 1984 to all dairy farms in the U.K, caused a hiccup or two, because the dairy farmers thought the milk quota should belong to them, but the law says that they only have the use of the quota while they are on that particular farm.

Although the dairy farmers produced the milk quota in the first place, the quota is attached to the surface of the land and belongs to no one, (the quota is what is called annexed to the soil). Dairy farmers however can sell the milk quota off their farms with land attached.

Now back to trespassing. How to prevent trespassing where no damage is proved is a somewhat difficult question.

The exasperating wooden notice-board is no preventive, or at most is merely an intimidation to the chicken–hearted, and there seems to be no sufficient remedy to deter any so minded loafer from wandering at will through your woods disturbing the game.

If you find a man walking through your woods doing no damage to trees, walls, or fences, your only course of action is to show him the quickest path to the Queen's highway and see that he takes it.

Should he object to going, then use as much force as is necessary 'only' and if he puts up a fight try to tie his hands, then have him tossed out of your wood. Remember, in defending yourself, use only enough force to evict the loafer from your wood.

If a man repeatedly trespasses after several warnings (which by the way had better be in writing), you can, if you like, bring an action and obtain an injunction against future trespassing. If he ignored the injunction then this would ensure he got a spell in prison for contempt of court.

However, owing to the expense, this is a remedy which would ordinarily be used only against a person of some means who could pay the costs.

Where, for instance, a neighbouring owner claims a right-of-way, which did not exist, through your field or wood, or the right to come on your land when shooting the boundary fence, this would be the course of action to take.

In cases like these an action for an injunction (which should not be brought until the trespass has been repeated several times) would be the appropriate remedy.

To deal with the ordinary trespasser who is generally a member of the public is another matter.

If he persists in continual trespassing then beyond turning him off there is no course open to you, except to set a watch on his movements and ascertain whether he does any damage, which will render him liable to prosecution.

If he is very careful, you must catch him by a trick. One way to do this is to manipulate a stile, so that when he enters your land the stile breaks when his weight is on it.

When you catch the trespasser breaking the stile you are then in a position to take him before the local bench of magistrates where a penalty is likely to be inflicted on him.

The common law allowed a man to do just what he liked to protect himself from intrusion. A man might set a trap to catch a trespasser, as he might to catch a thief.

He might (and may still) saw through the wooden bridge that crossed the little river flowing through his land and cause the trespasser to take a cold bath, without incurring

BROOM

any liability for doing so. Or, he might if he liked (and may still), dig a pit for the trespasser to fall into.

With regards however to spring-guns and man-traps and such like engines of war, a different law now prevails and these torture and maiming weapons, against man, have been outlawed.

A number of years ago I had the game and vermin shooting over some farm land which was split in two by a small strip of land which belonged to another man (let's call him Mr Short).

When I used to arrange to shoot over my own land with some friends I used to walk over the land nearest the farmhouse first which would take all morning.

Then, in the afternoon, we had quite a long walk, which took about half an hour or so to get round to the other part of the shoot. If we walked over Mr Short's land to get to the other part of the shoot it would only have taken us about five or ten minutes.

I knew quite well that Mr Short didn't like shooters and he wouldn't allow anybody to shoot over his land. I always walked the long way round with my friends to the second part of the shoot to prevent any trouble and to stop anyone from being embarrassed.

One day, however, I had arranged to go shooting with two of my friends, but unfortunately I had to call off at the last minute for business reasons. I told my friends just to go along on their own and have a bit of fun. Both friends had been shooting with me many times before and they knew the lie of the land and they knew my shooting boundaries.

THE KNAPWEED

It turned out to be a very wet day and in the afternoon

when they went to walk the second part of the shoot, because it was so wet, they thought they would take a short cut across Mr Short's land.

Mr Short caught them walking across his land and he was furious with them. He told them to get to hell off his land and don't ever come back on it again. (Mr Short's language was much stronger than what I can repeat).

My friends said both their guns were empty and they were just taking a short cut because it was so wet. Mr Short didn't see it like that and he gave my friends a rough time before they got smartly off his land.

A few days later I decided to visit Mr Short on his smallholding. I also decided to take him along a sweetener (a bottle of malt whisky), to try to smooth the passage and apologise to him for my friends trespassing over his land.

I knew who Mr Short was, but I had never met him before and I had heard that he was a bit short tempered. When I entered Mr Short's farm he was working in the yard.

I got out my car and walked over to Mr Short and introduced myself to him, but before I could apologise for my friends trespassing over his field. Mr Short blew his top (this is how it went on from there).

Mr Short said, 'So you are the B----- that trespasses over my land with your cronies. In future keep off my land, or I shall inform the police that you are poaching.'

He went on as to why couldn't I have had the decency to come and ask him in the first place, if I could walk over his land?

I managed to get a word in at this stage, and I said to Mr Short, as I handed him the carrier bag with a bottle of malt whisky in it, 'This is for the trouble my friends have caused and I want to apologise for them trespassing over your land.'

Mr Short took the bag with the whisky in it, but he never looked in the bag (he never even said thank you).

As Mr Short had simmered down a bit by then, I went on and told Mr Short that I had never walked over his land myself, and wouldn't do so without asking his permission first. Although, I said to him, that I was sometimes tempted to take a short cut.

Mr Short kept looking at me, as I went on to explain to him that to get to the second part of my shoot, it meant about half an hour's walk round the road, but if I could 'possibly' walk over his land it would only be a five minutes walk.

Mr Short was a good listener and he seemed very interested in what I had to say. I then asked him straight, if he would mind, if my friends and I walked over his field in the future to get to the other part of my shoot.

Mr Short was silent for a minute or so, as we kept an eye contact with each other. Then he said, 'Ah well I am sure you won't do any harm walking across my field.'

Mr Short and I then shook hands and we parted in a good frame of mind. From there on I used to drop the odd brace of pheasants into Mr Short, which kept the wheels well oiled and by being allowed to walk across his field very much improved my shoot.

TRESPASS IN PURSUIT OF GAME

The offence of trespassing in pursuit of game is dealt with chiefly by four statutes-the Night Poachers Act of 1828, the Game Act of 1831, the Night Poaching Act of 1844, and the Poaching Prevention Act of 1862. I shall try and address each of the Acts.

In ascertaining what is a trespass in pursuit of game, I must first have recourse to the words of the statutes themselves.

The Act of 1828 and the Act of 1831, deal respectively with the offence of night poaching and day poaching, and use practically the same words as to the trespass in describing several offences.

The Act of 1831 (sec 30) states, *if any person whatsoever shall commit any trespass by entering or being in the daytime upon any land in search or pursuit of game etc, etc.*

The Act of 1828 (sec 1) states, *if any person shall by night unlawfully enter or be in any land with any gun, for the purpose of taking or destroying game, etc, etc.*

It will be seen that the governing words in both Acts are *enter or to be.*

To commit a trespass within the meaning of these Acts a person must *enter* or *be* in or upon the land.

In this respect, the trespass dealt with by the Game Laws is slightly different and slightly less extensive, than trespass at common law.

At common law, as I have said, it is trespassing to wilfully throw a stone on to another man's land, or to fire a shot on to it.

Under these Acts, a personal entry is required. Some part of the body must be on, or over, land on which the person in question had no right to be. Any part of the body will do, stretching out an arm over the land is sufficient.

Personal entry is essential. It is not a trespass in pursuit of game if a man stands on land on which he has a right to be, and simply fires at game over land on which he has no right to be. Remember, this is the Game Act I am talking about.

It may be a common law trespass, and the shooter may be liable to an action at law, but it is not an offence punishable under the Game Act. So also it is no offence to send a dog on to land to range, with a view of driving the game over the boundary.

But, remember, it is a common law trespass to send your dog on to another man's land. However, with the Game Act of 1831 you can send your dog to range for game on another man's land, as long as you don't enter onto the land yourself, and with the view of the dog driving the game over your boundary.

In this connection, however, two rules of law must be borne in mind.

The first I would mention is that a man's right on the highway is limited to a right of passing along it in a lawful manner. He has no right to use a highway as a shooting ground any more than he has to play football on it.

As soon as he shoots (possibly as soon even as he has the intention to shoot), he becomes a trespasser.

Therefore, a man who fires at game from the highway over land where he has no right of shooting is guilty of a trespass in pursuit of game, and liable to be prosecuted.

He has *entered or been*, not on the land where the game was, but on the highway where he had no right to be, as he was not lawfully using it.

The second rule of law I would draw attention to is, that if the killing and picking up of the dead game follow close upon one another, or if, although not following closely there was at the time of killing the game an intention to take it when the opportunity offered, then the killing and subsequent entry to take the dead game are to be considered as one continuous act - trespass in pursuit of game.

Now there cannot be a trespass in pursuit of dead game, therefore, if a man sees a dead pheasant on his neighbour's land, and he goes on the land and picks it up (even although he had shot the pheasant the previous day), if he then had no intention of taking it, he is not guilty of trespass in pursuit of game, though he may be guilty of stealing.

If a man finds dead game or rabbits on another man's land and he takes them, he is guilty of larceny (stealing), and it makes no difference that the game or rabbits so found are some he shot himself the previous day, and did not at the time intend to pick them up.

So, it is a difficult question to distinguish an act which is larceny, from one which is a mere step, if I may use the expression, in the offence of trespass in pursuit of game.

This question of subsequent entry on the land in search of dead game previously killed by the searcher when standing on another man's land is well illustrated by a Court judgement in 1898.

In this case the defendant (let's call him Mr Wood), whilst standing in his allotment shot a grouse on the adjoining land over which Lord Westbury had the shooting rights.

FoxGLOVE

This was at 7 o'clock in the morning. Probably thinking he might be seen if he went after the bird then, Mr Wood left it and went away.

Soon afterwards Lord Westbury's keeper found the grouse, dead but still quite warm and he took it away. At 4.30 that afternoon Mr Wood was seen on the land looking for the grouse he had shot that morning.

He was promptly charged with the offence of trespass in pursuit in the daytime.

The justices found, as a fact, that Mr Wood was looking for the dead bird when he was seen on the land in the afternoon, but they refused to convict Mr Wood on the grounds that there could not be a trespass in pursuit of dead game.

A case for the opinion of the High Court. The Lord Chief Justice and Mr Justice Channell held that it was clearly a case in which Mr Wood ought to be convicted.

If Mr Wood had gone on the adjoining land in the afternoon on a 'fresh impulse' it would have been different, but the Justices, having found that he went to look for the bird he had previously shot, were bound to convict him and it did not matter that the dead bird had been removed previously.

From the above case Mr Wood might have learnt this moral:

He ought to have waited till night-time (i.e. more than an hour after sunset) before going to look for the bird, even if he had taken a lantern with him, for then (if he had found the bird) he couldn't have been convicted, (a) not of trespass in pursuit in the daytime, because entry was at night, and (b) not of night poaching, because the game was dead.

NAVIGABLE RIVERS

With regards, however, to the law on navigable rivers which are not tidal, that is, above the point to which the tide reaches, the law is different from that of the seashore.

Navigable rivers are public highways, it is true, but the beds of them and the water for the time being flowing above such beds belong, like the soil under the highway, to the private owners, usually the owners of the adjacent lands on either side.

The rights on such rivers are somewhat similar to those on a public road. Everyone has the right of sailing (rowing, steaming, etc.) over them, but the right of shooting belongs to the owners of the river bed, and any person endeavouring to take game on a non-tidal river renders himself liable to a prosecution for trespass in pursuit of game.

As an instance of trespass in pursuit of game on a navigable river, I shall try and explain and give you short details of a case which came before a bench of magistrates in Norfolk some time ago.

It must first be stated that, under the Summary of the Jurisdiction Act of 1848, that every person who *aids and abets* in any offence punishable in a court is himself liable to similar prosecution and punishment.

The defendant in this case (let's call him Mr Ord) was summoned for aiding and abetting a person unknown in the commission of a trespass in pursuit of game on one of the Norfolk rivers.

Mr Ord was a 'mate' on a small boat, which had apparently been hired, by a party of gentlemen, for a week's cruise on the Broads.

The chief, and only, witness for the prosecution was a gamekeeper, who said that when in a wood at some little distance from the river he heard a shot being fired on the river, and coming at once out of the wood he ran down to the bank.

On his way he said he saw a gentleman, who was evidently one of the party on board, standing at the stern of the boat with a gun under his arm, apparently speaking to the mate.

As the keeper approached the river, the gentleman with the gun went below, and the mate got into a small jolly boat and rowed to the farther bank, where he picked up, either on the land or from the water, something which the keeper swore was a pheasant, and rowed back to the boat with it.

The keeper at once went to the boathouse nearby, and rowed down after the boat, upon reaching the boat he had a heated conversation with the skipper and his mate, who assured him that the bird shot was a coot, which he held up for him to see.

The keeper subsequently made inquires of the owner of the boat, with a view of ascertaining the identity of the gentleman who fired the shot.

Information on this point was however, refused, and the keeper accordingly had to content himself with prosecuting the mate of the boat as an aider and abetter.

The only evidence that could be in favour of Mr Ord was that the skipper of the vessel was his father and he swore positively that he had never seen a pheasant and that the bird Mr Ord picked up was in fact a coot.

The magistrates, however, disbelieved this story, and the question was whether there was a good case in law against Mr Ord.

The solicitor for the prosecution quoted an old case, the facts of which were: Mr A was driving in his own cart along a country road and picked up Mr B and gave him a ride.

Mr B had a gun with him, and when they arrived opposite a certain wood Mr A stopped the cart and Mr B got down and went into the wood and shot a hare and brought it back. He got back onto the cart and was driven by Mr A to the next village.

Mr A was prosecuted for aiding and abetting Mr B in trespassing in pursuit of game, and the judges of the High Court held that the magistrates were justified in convicting Mr A

The Ord case is very similar. For the defence it was argued that Mr Ord (the mate on the boat) wouldn't admit to the shooting of the pheasant (if it was a pheasant that was shot), and there can be no trespass in pursuit of dead game, and so Mr Ord had committed no offence under the Act.

The magistrates, however, decided otherwise and by a majority convicted Mr Ord for trespass in pursuit of game in the daytime and he was fined £2.

The Poacher's Lawyer considered the case carefully at the time it was reported in the newspapers and he came to the conclusion that the magistrates had made a mistake (as even magistrates will at times).

The lawyer thought that the magistrates had unduly stretched the law in order to punish someone for an offence which they did not doubt had been committed, but the real offender had escaped identification.

Granted said the lawyer that the case quoted by the advocate for the prosecution (about Mr A and the hare case) this was good law, but it is distinctly different from the one under consideration.

In the hare case it was pretty clear that Mr A, the driver of the cart, rendered, to some extent, an assistance to Mr B before the offence was committed, he was party to the premeditation.

In the Mr Ord case, however, the offence was complete, as far as the man who fired the shot was concerned, before Mr Ord got into the boat and rowed to the far bank.

Now, said the lawyer, it is quite clear that if someone on another boat had shot the pheasant, and had sailed on without troubling to pick it up, and Mr Ord in the other boat had seen the dead bird and rowed out and picked it up for himself, he would not have been guilty of any offence under the Game Act, although his act might have amounted to stealing.

How, then, could it make any difference that the man who shot the pheasant was in the same boat as Mr Ord who picked it up?

Mr Ord was not shown to have had any conversation with the shooter before the shot was fired. Had there been any evidence of that kind, the case would have assumed a different aspect.

As it was, the lawyer couldn't but think that the magistrates would have been justified in refusing to convict Mr Ord.

The case, however, is interesting as it shows that the magistrates of Norfolk (most of them landowners and sportsmen) will do their utmost to put down the shooting of game upon the rivers and broads, which are generally asserted to be tidal waters.

Chapter 10   CLOSE TIMES, MANORS & WARRENS

The close season for most wild game birds and animals is in the summer. This is to let these creatures breed and produce a new generation of young.

There are many other factors involved with the reproduction and the survival of many young wild birds and animals in the countryside. The weather, poaching, the stealing of game birds, and the eggs from birds of prey.

The weather can and does play the greatest part in the reproduction of wild birds and animals in the countryside. Take the grouse for instance, these birds live out on the hills and moors all the year round no matter what the weather is like.

Up in the north I have witnessed some very hard winters with very heavy falls of snow and hard frosts. I have followed and studied the behaviour of the red grouse during one or two arctic winters in the north.

The arctic winter killed off a great number of the red grouse due to starvation. The weak and the old birds were first to die. Some of the grouse came right down from the hills and moors to the country villages looking for food.

I even saw some grouse near a town sitting up in a hawthorn bush eating the berries. This was starvation behaviour by the grouse.

This particular year was 1963 and it was a dreadful winter. Many thousands of small birds died from lack of food that winter. Although the countryside soon recovered in the spring of the following year, the wild bird and animal population was sadly reduced.

During some hard winters I have seen the snow lying in drifts up to seven or eight metres high in some places. The harder the winter the more effect it has on the wild bird and animal population.

Vermin, such as stoats, weasels, foxes, cats, rats and birds of prey all play a part in reducing the wild bird and animal population, but not to the extent that any species will become extinct.

Vermin and birds of prey keep a fairly good balance in the countryside. It is only when man interferes, or changes the environment, that a drastic effect will be made on the wild bird and animal population.

There are not nearly the number of small birds in the towns, cities and the countryside nowadays. The main causes are the changes in agriculture and the changes in our towns and cities.

In the countryside, for instance, the corncrake has nearly disappeared, except for small pockets of them in the far north of Scotland and in Ireland. The modern grass cutting machine is the main cause for the loss of the corncrake, because this machine cuts so close to the ground that it just chops everything up.

Silage making also helped to push the corncrake from the land, as the first cut of grass for silage is made earlier, and the wild birds like the corncrake, the pheasant and the partridges are already sitting on eggs and are just chopped to pieces.

The use of pesticides has also had some effect on the wild bird population. I think pesticides have a bigger effect on the insect population than on the wild bird population, although I am well aware that most wild birds, especially the young ones, need insects for the first ten days of their lives and it's the lack of insects that kills many young chicks.

On the farms in the 1950's and 1960's there used to be plenty of grain lying about in the farm buildings during the summer and winter. There were also stubble fields on the farms right through the winter and these provided a supply of food for a great variety of small and large birds all the year round, including birds of prey.

There were also plenty of rats and mice about the farms. Today much of the grain stored on farms is in metal bins, or containers, and the wild birds like house and tree sparrows, finches and tits can't get at the grain so they leave the farm.

The barn owl is a good example. This beautiful bird of prey has been driven off most farms, because its accommodation and its food supply are no longer there, but most important of all, it is because most of the old barns have either been pulled down to make way for bigger buildings, or they have been converted into houses.

Some of the new modern asbestos, or metal sheeting farm building are cold and draughty and wild birds don't like these sorts of places, and when there is less grain and fewer rats and mice around the birds scarper. Wild birds like to be cosy and warm (pheasants for instance don't like dark cold woods with no ground cover).

In the towns and cities there are fewer small birds about in the daytime. Again the main cause is the shortage of nesting places and the shortage of food.

About twenty five years ago there were still horses working in the cities pulling brewery carts etc. and there was always plenty of grain lying about for the birds to feed on; it was the same at the docks, where there were always plenty of rats, mice and meal for them to find.

At one time, at most creameries, mills, bakeries, industrial sites, docks and stables there were plenty of open buildings. Many of the buildings in our towns, cities and at the docks have been closed, pulled down, or converted into offices and

houses, and there are now fewer open buildings for the daytime birds to feed and nest in. .

So what we now have is millions of wild birds that only use the towns and cities to roost in at night, like the starlings and the pigeons, and they have become a nuisance.

The greed of man is to blame for our not seeing so many songbirds about today. Man and machines have changed our countryside, towns and cities.

Some people, though, put more into the countryside than they take from it.

For instance, the game shooters put a great deal more into the countryside than they take from it, because when they feed their pheasants and partridges, they also feed thousands of small and large wild birds at the same time, and during a very hard winter many of these wild birds will be saved from starvation by the game shooters.

Now let us look at the close seasons. You can ask any game shooter when the grouse and pheasant shooting season starts and they will tell you straight away without giving it a second thought; but if you ask the same shooters when the close seasons are for the same game birds they will have to stop and think.

It may perhaps be advisable to say a few words about this. The regulations as to the close times, however, are so very clearly defined that there are but few loopholes.

The close times for England, as defined by the Game Act of 1831 (Section 3), are as follows.

For all 'game' (which of course includes hares), Sunday and Christmas day every year.

(1) For pheasants from 1st February to 1st October.

(2) For partridge from 1st February to 1st September.

(3) For grouse from 10th December to 12th August.

The Game Act of 1830 seems to allow a poacher or loafer to take pot shots at game birds in the close season, as long as they don't kill or take them.

Although to create the offence last considered the game must be 'killed or taken', it is not necessary of course that it should be shot, or even killed.

To take a pheasant alive in the close season is just as much an offence as to shoot it. Even where a pheasant is accidentally caught in a wire, and the occupier takes it out alive, he may not kill it or even take it away with the object of killing it (Wakins v Price 1878).

It would almost seem as if the catching of wild pheasants for their eggs and to enclose them in pens, as is done on many sporting estates, was within the letter of the law.

The judge laid it down in the last named case (in effect) that the taking of a pheasant, with the object of subsequently restoring it to its freedom, was not an offence.

With regards to Sundays and Christmas Days, the law is different. Not only is the killing or taking unlawful, but the penalties of the Act are incurred *by using any dog, gun, net, or other engine, or instrument for the purpose of killing or taking any game.*

It has been decided that a snare is an *engine* within the meaning of the Act. Moreover, the snare need not be actually set on the Sunday to render the offence liable. If it is set on

139

Friday or Saturday, and left in its place on Sunday, with the intention of catching any hare that may happen to go into it, the setter is liable to the penalty of not exceeding £5 and costs (Allen v Thompson) 1870.

It would seem, from this decision, that no one has a right to keep snares set week in and week out. To be absolutely safe the setter must take them up every Saturday before midnight, and reset them again after midnight on Sunday.

Of course, if a snare is set for rabbits and a hare is caught by accident, no offence is committed, but if the hare is taken before it is killed it must be released, and there may be some difficulty in satisfying a bench of magistrates, in some cases, that the snare was set for rabbits and not for hares.

PHEASANT IN BRANDY SAUCE

You either like the taste of game or you don't. All types of game have a particularly strong taste, and it is what is done with the game that can make it as attractive to eat and enjoy as any other types of meat.

I prefer wild duck to any other type of game myself, although I eat pheasant and grouse from time to time, but duck to me in a black cherry or orange sauce is delicious and can be served with any vegetables.

Game needs to be hung up for a week or ten days to tenderise the meat and to help to bring out the flavour. Like most meats they have to mature. Take beef, for instance, the longer it hangs the more tender it will become.

When you go into the butcher's shop for a joint of beef look for a joint that is fairly dark, this will tell you that the meat has been hanging for some time and it should therefore be lovely and tender.

My mother always used to say it is the cook that makes the meat tender. If we ever sat down to a tough bit of meat or steak, my mother would say it is not the meat, it is the cook's fault that the meat is tough.

An old aunt of mine used to cook her meats on a paraffin stove, she also made soup on the same stove. What a great cook she was, you never ever got a bit of tough meat in her house, and her soup, like my mother's, was a meal on its own.

When we are out pheasant shooting, some birds get damaged more than others from the shot, or they hit a tree or stone wall when falling, or some dogs, if they are a bit hard in the mouth, can also badly damage game.

When we come to sort out the dead game at the end of the day, the very badly damaged pheasants are laid aside and the guests are given a brace of good pheasants (one would never dream of giving a guest damaged birds).

The damaged pheasants are then hung up for a few days and are used for providing the lunch on the next shooting day.

This is how my wife makes 'Pheasant in Brandy Sauce'. A delicious lunch on a cold day, or any day.

The pheasants are first dressed out, then they are boiled until the meat is tender. The meat is then taken off the bone and put into a casserole dish. Take one ounce of margarine, one ounce of flour, top of the milk, a shake of Worcester sauce, a shake of tomato ketchup, a shake of black pepper, a pinch of gravy salt and add brandy to taste.

Melt the margarine and mix flour and gravy salt, then add the pheasant stock and milk, put in black pepper, Worcester sauce and tomato ketchup. Add brandy to taste, pour over pheasant and heat in the oven. Serve with mashed creamed potatoes and garden peas. Follow this with hot home made mince pies, take the top off the pies and pour one dessert spoonful of brandy over mince meat, serve with fresh runny cream. Finish with a glass of brandy (delicious any time).

MANORS

Lords of manors and their gamekeepers have certain rights and privileges not shared by ordinary owners or occupiers of land and their gamekeepers.

A manor or lordship, be it known, is what the law calls an incorporeal hereditament, comprising of more or less absolute rights of jurisdiction over a district, the whole of which was the property of the first lord of the manor, who granted parts out to tenants to cultivate, while reserving his own land, and also the wastes over which tenants were given a right to graze sheep or cattle.

Every manor had its baronial court for the trial of disputes and for providing the punishment of offences.

The manor tenants would meet yearly in many cases in a convenient public-house, where the steward would receive the yearly rents and he would provide refreshments for the tenants.

The wastes of the manor belong to the lord, and he has the right of the game thereon.

These wastes may be common lands, on which the tenants, or some of them, have rights to graze sheep or cattle, or they may be called absolute wastes, such as the foreshore of the sea or an estuary, where such foreshore has been granted to the lord by the Crown.

By the Game Act of 1831 the lord of any manor is authorised to appoint one or more persons to serve as gamekeepers to kill game on the manor.

By Section 13 of the Act, the gamekeepers on the manor can also seize and take for the use of the lord all such *dogs, nets, and other engines or instruments for the killing of game* from any person who has no licence to kill game.

The section quoted does not authorise the seizure of guns, but only of dogs, nets, or other engines or instruments, such for instance as snares, and they must be used for the purpose of taking game (not rabbits or woodcock etc). It is only while guns are being so used, or immediately afterwards that they can be seized.

It seems that the lord's gamekeeper may shoot an unlicensed person's dog which is being used for the purpose of taking game within the manor, though an ordinary gamekeeper would not have this power (Kingsworth v Bretton) 1814.

A lord of the manor, or his gamekeeper may arrest any person found committing an offence under the Night Poachers Act of 1828, within limits of the manor (Section 2).

The gamekeeper may also demand to see the licence of any person found taking or pursuing game within the manor (Game Licence Act, (Section 10)). Further, under section 35, either the lord or his gamekeeper may demand any game recently killed by a person found trespassing in pursuit by day or night. If refused he may seize the game.

Again, a lord of the manor and his gamekeeper are exempt from the provisions against trespassers in pursuit of game in the daytime, contained in the Game Act of 1831 (Section 35), as far as the limits of the manor are concerned. Which means the lord of the manor could almost do as he wanted with a trespasser within the manor.

The ancient rights, however, of lords of manors with the sporting rights over the wastes and common lands, have in the great majority of cases been lost by the enclosure of these lands under the various Enclosure Acts.

To ascertain whether the lord of the manor has a right of sporting over lands enclosed and allotted to tenants of the manor, one must look at the Special Enclosure Act, and see how the awards were made by the Enclosure Commissioners.

All, or most, of the local Acts contain certain reservations for the lord of the manor, but it depends on the wording of the clause of the reservation whether the right of sporting over lands to be enclosed are lost or not.

With regards to commons, the soil of which is vested in the lord of the manor, the commoners merely have the right of pasture and the sporting rights remain with the lord. It was stated in one old case that commoners may, for the protection of their grass, destroy rabbits which come on to the common from other land, not being the lord's land (Cooper v Marshall).

This ruling seems to be somewhat inconsistent with the recognised principle that, as soon as animals such as hares or rabbits come upon any land, the right to take them belongs to the owner of the soil, unless such rights has been transferred to another person.

This means that commoners have the right to take hares and rabbits if they are eating their grass, but the hares and rabbits must not be coming from the lord's land. Where else can they come from if the surrounding land belongs to the lord and he has the sporting rights over his land?

Moreover, it has been clearly laid down that if the lord likes to make a rabbit-burrow on the common, or to encourage the breeding of hares and rabbits, the commoners have no right to destroy either the rabbits or hares, or to block or destroy the burrows.

If, however, by the lord of the manor's act, the rabbits so increase as to destroy the pasture of the common, then this is becomes a surcharge of the common, and any commoner may bring an action at law in order to restrain him, in the same way as he would bring a similar action against another commoner, for putting too many sheep or cattle on the common.

WARRENS

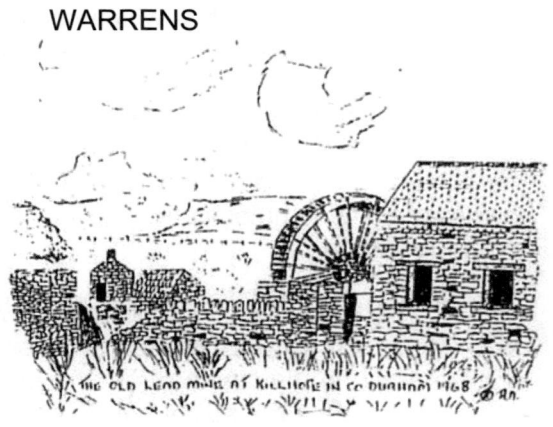

Perhaps it was in order to encourage the breeding of hares and rabbits for sale that special provisions were inserted into the Larceny Act of 1861, giving additional protection to the owners of 'rabbit warrens' against both day and night poachers and loafers.

Any grounds set apart for the breeding of hares or rabbits, whether enclosed or not, constitutes a 'warren' within the Act.

To take hares or rabbits from a warren is, of course an offence against the Game Laws, constituting either a trespass in pursuit of game, or night poaching, according to the time at which the offence is committed.

However, the Larceny Act creates additional offences, making it a misdemeanour triable and punishable by a fine or imprisonment, to take or kill at night any hare or rabbit in any warren on land lawfully set apart for a breeding ground (night being the first hour after sunset to the beginning of the last hour before sunrise).

To take or kill a hare or rabbit in the daytime, or to set a snare or trap in a warren at any time, is an offence punishable before the magistrates and a fine not exceeding £5 (Section 17).

Anyone may have a rabbit warren on his land, he may turn down rabbits and encourage them to make their earths all in the same place. Which, for instance could be in an old sandpit, or in an old quarry, by enclosing the land temporarily or by other means. His neighbours may shoot the rabbits if they stray onto their land, but not, of course, otherwise.

The neighbours, however have no right to redress at law against the incursions of the rabbits into their crops. The answer of the warren owner to any such complaint is. 'You should put some wire netting round your field to stop them.'

Every farmer has to fence against his own stock, but he needn't fence against rabbits in his warrens if he keeps them and, as shown in Boulston's case, no action can be brought against him for keeping them.

In that case, it was stated that if a man makes rabbit burrows in his own land, which increase in so great numbers that they destroy his neighbour's land next adjoining, his neighbour cannot have an action against him for making the rabbit burrows. However, if the rabbits go onto the neighbour's land he can shoot them.

There is, however, another aspect to this case, for the land may be so artificially stocked with rabbits as to give the adjoining owner a right of action.

Finally the following is a case where some land had been over stocked with rabbits,.

A young man had been experimenting with a rabbit farm with which he had some success. He went to consult *The Poachers Lawyer* one fine summer morning.

This young man, lets call him Mr Farmer, had of course, as is usual on rabbit farms, close fencing or wire netting all round the land and he kept a very large stock of rabbits.

As Mr Farmer walked into the lawyer's office, he began. 'You know my rabbit farm? Well somehow or other, a bit of the wire netting got knocked down last night and about a hundred and fifty of my rabbits got out.'

The lawyer knew Mr Farmer and was quite friendly with him. The lawyer said, 'Well my dear fellow, you surely haven't come to me to catch them for you, or to tell you how to catch them, have you?'

Mr Farmer said, 'No, no. Anybody can catch and kill them if they like. I can put up with losing that number of rabbits; but you know old Mr Bates has got the farm next to my land and, as luck would have it, this breakdown of my fence happened just opposite a very promising field of his wheat, and all my rabbits are in it. Mr Bates has been down to my house in a towering rage, and he says the rabbits will eat the whole crop before long. I am not liable as you said, but it is beastly awkward.'

The lawyer said, 'Hold on there, who said you weren't liable?'

Mr Farmer replied, 'Well you said the governor wasn't liable for the rabbits in the warren, and it's all the same isn't it?'

The lawyer advised, 'Not quite my friend, you see your father really only caused the rabbits to live and breed in the gravel-pit in a state of nature. He started them and they did the rest. They made their homes themselves, but you have brought on to your land an enormous number of rabbits beyond what would naturally live there, as is proved by the fact that you have to keep them in by a fence.'

The lawyer went on, 'Now it is settled law that if a man brings on to his land something which, if let loose, would do damage, whether it is water in a reservoir or a lion in a cage, he must take the fullest responsibility for it, if it gets loose from any cause whatever, and he is liable to his neighbour for any damage done.'

Mr Farmer said, 'But I didn't knock the fence down. Somebody came in the night and did it for spite.'

The lawyer replied, 'That again doesn't matter, unless it was Mr Bates himself, or somebody acting by his orders. You have chosen to bring and extraordinary number of rabbits on to your farm and the law treats them the same as dangerous animals. I am afraid you will have to pay Mr Bates. However, if you can find out who knocked the fence down prosecute him, by all means, or if he is worth it, sue him for the damage you yourself have to pay, and also for the value of the rabbits, but first of all go straight along to Mr Bates and try and settle at once for as low a figure you can. If you can't do it for a reasonable figure, come to me and I will try.'

Mr Farmer, acting on the advice from the lawyer, managed to settle the matter amicably with Mr Bates without any Court action.